The Knots in English

The Knots in English
A Manual for Caribbean Users

MERLE HODGE

IAN RANDLE PUBLISHERS
Kingston • Jamaica

First edition 1997, Calaloux Publications

First Published in Jamaica, 2011 by
Ian Randle Publishers
11 Cunningham Avenue
P.O. Box 686
Kingston 6
www.ianrandlepublishers.com

© 2011 Merle Hodge

Cataloguing in Publication data available from the National Library of Jamaica.

ISBN 978-976-637-526-3 (pbk)

All rights reserved. No part of this publication may be reproduced, stored in a retrieval system or transmitted in any form or by an means electronic, photocopying, recording or otherwise, without the prior permission of the publisher and author.

Cover and book design by Ian Randle Publishers

Printed in the United States of America

Dedicated to

Liris Armstrong and Jean Pearse

Contents

Preface   xi

BASICS

A   Word Classes (or "The Parts of Speech")
A1	Nouns	3
A2	Pronouns	5
A3	Adjectives	8
A4	Verbs	11
A5	Adverbs	16
A6	Prepositions	19
A7	Conjunctions	22
A8	Interjections	23
A9	Word classes/Word slots	24

B   The Sentence
B1	What is a sentence?	30
B2	The subject	32
B3	The object	34
B4	The indirect object	37
B5	The complement	39
B6	Phrases and clauses	42

NOUN FORMS

C   Number
C1	Singular and plural	51
C2	Different ways of adding **s**	52
C3	Other plural forms	54
C4	Plural markers: Creole v. English	56
C5	Countable and uncountable nouns	58
C6	Use of determiners	60
C7	Articles: when to use **an**	65
C8	Nouns with quantity expressions	67
C9	One of. . .	71

	C10	Nouns ending with a sound like **s**	73
	C11	Some problem nouns	74

D Possession

	D1	Forming the possessive	77
	D2	Forming the possessive with **of**	80
	D3	The possessive: common errors	83
	D4	Possessive nouns v. adjectival nouns	86

VERB FORMS

E The Present Simple Tense

	E1	Forming the present simple tense	91
	E2	Uses of the present simple tense	93
	E3	When to put the **s**	95
	E4	The present tense: Creole influence	99
	E5	The verb **to be**	101
	E6	Identifying the head word	105
	E7	Present tense verbs in joined sentences	110
	E8	Verb before subject	112
	E9	There is/are	113
	E10	Relative pronoun as subject	115
	E11	Subjects with quantity expressions	119
	E12	Verbs ending with a sound like **s**	124
	E13	Unchangeable noun as subject	125
	E14	Question form of the present simple tense	128
	E15	Negative form of the present simple tense	132
	E16	Double negatives	136
	E17	Present simple tense: Negative questions	140
	E18	Where not to put the **s**	142
	E19	The verb **to be**: Question form	148
	E20	The verb **to be**: Negative form	151
	E21	The verb **to be**: Negative questions	154

F The Past Simple Tense

	F1	Forming the past simple tense	156
	F2	Verbs which do not change	160

	F3	Past tense verbs in joined sentences	161
	F4	Verbs ending with a sound like **d**	163
	F5	Question form of the past simple tense	164
	F6	Negative form of the past simple tense	166
	F7	When not to use past tense form	168
	F8	The verb **to be**: Past simple tense	173
	F9	**Were** in if-clauses	178
	F10	**Could** and **would**	179
G	**The Past Participle**		
	G1	Identifying the past participle	190
	G2	The past participle as adjective	192
	G3	The present perfect tense	197
	G4	The past perfect tense	202
	G5	The passive voice	208
	G6	Notable past participles	215
	G7	Verbs ending with **d**, **t**, or **en**	220
H	**The Present Participle**		
	H1	The present participle as noun and adjective	223
	H2	The continuous tenses	227
	H3	Confusing the participles	232
Answers			239
Index			274

Preface

This text addresses the specific problems which people in the "English-speaking" Caribbean have with learning the official language.

The majority of us are not, of course, English-speaking. We are a Creole-speaking people. We have a language of our own, and English is another language that we have to learn.

The trouble is that we are not always able to distinguish Creole from English. This is because we use the same words in Creole as in English: both have more or less the same vocabulary. Often people assume that they are speaking or writing English because they are using English words.

However, our first language (or "mother tongue") has a different grammar from English, a different sound system and a certain percentage of its vocabulary that is not English.

This manual focuses on those areas of English grammar that are different from Creole grammar. Those are the areas in which Caribbean people most frequently produce errors when they are using English. We are liable to make mistakes because English is not our mother tongue, and like the Venezuelan or Guadeloupean using English, we may take something of our mother tongue with us when we cross over into another language.

We are less likely to make those mistakes if we are aware of the differences between English and Creole. This book aims at helping Caribbean people see those differences more clearly.

Learning English does not mean unlearning Creole. The aim of the book is to help its users improve their English language proficiency. At the same time, however, it is hoped that Caribbean users will gain from it a greater respect for their mother tongue as a language in its own right.

The Knots in English comes out of twenty-five years of language arts teaching in different parts of the Caribbean and at different levels of the education system — the secondary school, the teachers' college, the university. There is great consistency in the types of problems that crop up in the English produced by people over a wide span of Caribbean populations, and this is because the basic structure of our mother tongue is the same, from the Guyanas to the Bahamas.

The Knots In English

The manual is aimed at students in the upper levels of the education system — secondary school students from about Form 4 upwards, and university students who show serious deficiencies in their mastery of English, as evidenced by the high failure rate in the English language courses required by most faculties of the University of the West Indies.

It also offers help to teachers, who are by and large thrown into English language teaching without being equipped with a sufficient knowledge of the workings of either the language to be taught or the first language of their students.

Knots can also be used as a reference text by people who have long passed through the education system but who feel that their knowledge of English could be improved. Media workers in particular are increasingly under attack from members of the public who complain of "falling standards" in the use of English in the media.

Level 1 of *The Knots in English* comprises eight sections, A–H, broken down into 71 sub-sections, each addressing a specific grammar point.

The two introductory sections, A and B, are meant to provide a general foundation by explaining the roles that words play and how they are put together into English sentences.

Then the manual focuses on the behaviour of nouns and verbs in English. A major problem area for Creole speakers is the use of the word-endings which in English indicate changes in the functions of nouns and verbs.

Explanations of grammar points may include looking at the Creole rule as well as the English rule. These explanations refer to two varieties of Creole — Trinidadian and Jamaican.

Although the basic structure of Creole is the same across the Caribbean, the region can be sub-divided into two groups of Creole speakers with differences in certain details of their grammar. These differences can be pinpointed by comparing Trinidadian speech to Jamaican speech. The speech of different Caribbean populations shows features of the one or the other. The language of Tobago, for example, is of the Jamaican type, not the Trinidadian, although Trinidad and Tobago are one country.

Where examples of Creole are given, mostly English spelling is used. This does not convey the pronunciation of Creole, but Caribbean users of the manual will know how to pronounce the words which they read in a Creole sentence.

Preface

The manual is structured in such a way that it can be used either as a reference text or a teaching text. Users may either consult individual sections for clarification on particular grammar points, or work through the sections from beginning to end. The content is broken down and sequenced in such a manner that the manual can be used as a course. Sub-sections build upon each other, and explanations are followed by practice assignments for which answers are provided in a separate section. No answers are given for substitution tables, such as assignment 1 on page 98, or open assignments, such as 2. and 3. on the same page.

It is important to note that not all of our problems with the use of English are to be blamed on Creole. Level 2 of *The Knots in English* (to appear at a later date) will address, among other things, problems of sentence construction which are really problems of anybody who does not do enough reading. Many native speakers of English (Americans and British people, for example) make some of these same errors in composing sentences.

In the long run all the English grammar books in the world cannot teach you English unless you also do a great deal of reading. Learning the grammar is only part of learning a language. You also need to develop a wide vocabulary. Reading will help you do both—master the grammar and build up a large stock of words and expressions which you know how to use accurately and appropriately.

The main objective of this work is to provide support for the teaching and learning of English in the Caribbean language situation. It is hoped, however, that it will also provide its Caribbean users with a new understanding of their own language, thereby making some contribution to Caribbean self-knowledge.

Many thanks to Barbara Lalla for her very helpful review, and to all the other people who by their vote of confidence helped this work come into being, especially Helen Pyne-Timothy, Denis Solomon, Valerie Youssef, Paula Morgan, and Selwyn Cudjoe.

Merle Hodge

Basics

A. Word Classes or "The Parts of Speech"

1. **In every language, sounds combine to form words, and words combine to form sentences.**
   Sentences are **organized** groups of words working together to express thoughts. In this "organization", words fill different positions, or play different roles.

2. **Words are divided into different classes according to the work they do in a sentence.**
   There are eight of these **word classes**, also called the **parts of speech**:

   Nouns, Pronouns, Adjectives, Verbs, Adverbs, Prepositions, Conjunctions, Interjections.

AI NOUNS

1. In the following passage, all the words in bold type are nouns:

Disaster

When she thought it might be safe, **Sylvie** crept nervously out of the **house** to see the **damage**. She could not believe her **eyes**.

There was **destruction** everywhere. **Sylvie** suddenly wanted to run back into the **safety** of the strong, old **building**, but she checked herself. She stood on the **step** and stared in **horror**.
5 The **sight** made her dizzy.

The **hurricane** had ripped off the **roofs** of **neighbours' houses**. It had twisted **pieces** of **metal** into strange **shapes**. It had torn up large **trees** by their **roots** and flung them down again. Some **houses** had become crazy **heaps** of **timber**.

People were very cautiously coming out to stare at the **town**. **Aruna** seemed like a different
10 **place**. It was almost unrecognizable.

Sylvie felt weak.

---

2. Nouns name things, people, places or ideas.

The Knots In English

AI Practice

1. Put one word in each blank space below.

If these sentences then make sense, the words you have put in are **nouns**.

A. (a) The _____ was damaged in the accident.
   (b) Gloria, _____ and Savitri voted against.
   (c) While all this was going on, a large grey _____ suddenly appeared out of nowhere.
   (d) The manager reported that three _____ had already resigned.
   (e) Marley's _____ will be held on the third of June.

B. (a) She saw a _____ next door.
   (b) The public health authorities have closed down this _____ because of malfunctioning toilets.
   (c) We found Jerry's _____ a few days later.
   (d) That story lacks _____ .
   (e) They were throwing empty _____ everywhere.

C. (a) When decisions are taken by the _____, they should be implemented without any _____.
   (b) Those people are soon going to find themselves in a difficult _____.
   (c) This airline plies the route from Kingston to _____ which is the capital of _____.
   (d) The students received an award for their outstanding _____.
   (e) After some _____, the date of the _____ was announced.

D. (a) There is a _____ in the water.
   (b) In 1930 there were no _____ in this district.
   (c) Staring me right in the face was a vicious-looking _____.
   (d) On the far side of the hill stands a _____.
   (e) Where are my _____?

2. Find the nouns in the following sentences:

A. (a) The police arrested two suspects.
   (b) The newspapers were not allowed to publish their names.

(c) They appeared in court on Wednesday.
(d) The lawyer representing them was Barbara Davis.
(e) Their case was adjourned to a date in February.

B. (a) Trevor and Naima entered the race this year.
(b) The marathon is an annual event.
(c) They trained for months before the day.
(d) They became very fit and both were able to run the whole distance.
(e) Neither Trevor nor Naima won any prize, but they thoroughly enjoyed the experience.

C. (a) Our panside celebrates its tenth anniversary next week.
(b) The name of the band is Panthers.
(c) All of our members live in LaGrange or in communities nearby.
(d) The celebration will be held in the savannah.
(e) There will be food, drinks, games and, above all, music.

Answers p. 239

A2 PRONOUNS

1. Below, all the words in bold type are pronouns:

Disaster

When **she** thought **it** might be safe, Sylvie crept nervously out of the house to see the damage. **She** could not believe **her** eyes.

There was destruction everywhere. Sylvie suddenly wanted to run back into the safety of the strong, old building, but **she** checked **herself**. **She** stood on the step and stared in horror.
5   The sight made **her** dizzy.

The hurricane had ripped off the roofs of neighbours' houses. **It** had twisted pieces of metal into strange shapes. **It** had torn up large trees by **their** roots and flung **them** down again. Some houses had become crazy heaps of timber.

People were very cautiously coming out to stare at the town. Aruna seemed like a different
10 place. **It** was almost unrecognizable.

Sylvie felt weak.

2. Pronouns usually refer to things, people, places or ideas without naming them.

In the passage above:

– the pronouns **she, her** and **herself** refer to Sylvie.

– the pronoun **it** in line 1 refers to the action of going outdoors, to the hurricane in lines 6 and 7, and to Aruna in line 10.

– in line 7 the pronouns **their** and **them** refer to the trees.

3. Here is a list of the most common pronouns:

I, me, my, mine, myself

you, your, yours, yourself, yourselves

she, her, hers, herself

he, him, his, himself

it, its, itself

we, us, our, ours, ourselves

they, them, their, theirs, themselves

who, whom, which

that, this, these, those

one, one's, some, any, none

someone, everyone, anyone

somebody, nobody, everybody, anybody

something, nothing, everything, anything

A2 Practice

1. Replace the nouns in bold type by the right pronouns:

   (a) **Jacqueline** is having an asthma attack.

   (b) We found the **papers** in an old cardboard box.

   (c) Those people will get a reply from **George** when he comes back.

   (d) As the alcohol wore off, Roland became **Roland** again.

   (e) You should have seen **Marjorie's** face when she heard the news.

2. Identify the pronouns in each sentence below. Then replace each by another pronoun, for example:

   > I made a bottle of rum punch yesterday.

   The pronoun is **I**.

   > You made a bottle of rum punch yesterday.

   I is replaced by **you**.

A. (a) We assembled at the foot of the hill.

   (b) After three days she still had not returned.

   (c) Please tell me whether that is too close to the wall.

   (d) Somebody will have to work out a solution.

   (e) Finally they began to see signs of progress.

B. (a) Mr Barnes controls everything.

   (b) St Mary's beat us in the first game.

   (c) The court will settle yours in about two months' time.

   (d) Children prefer these.

   (e) The whole incident has really embarrassed her a great deal.

C. (a) Anil had to go back for it.

   (b) Grace is talking to herself again.

   (c) The secretary can make contact with them by tomorrow.

   (d) People placed their confidence in him from the very first day of the campaign.

   (e) The photographer took a picture of that for the records.

D. (a) Their chickens are roaming all over the place.
   (b) The driver found my briefcase on the bus.
   (c) New locks were installed at his request.
   (d) There is a bus stop quite close to our house.
   (e) Its aims are clearly stated.

Answers p. 239

A3 ADJECTIVES

1. Here all the words in bold type are adjectives:

Disaster

When she thought it might be **safe**, Sylvie crept nervously out of the house to see the damage. She could not believe her eyes.

There was destruction everywhere. Sylvie suddenly wanted to run back into the safety of the **strong**, **old** building, but she checked herself. She stood on the step and stared in horror.
5 The sight made her **dizzy**.

The hurricane had ripped off the roofs of neighbours' houses. It had twisted pieces of metal into **strange** shapes. It had torn up **large** trees by their roots and flung them down again. Some houses had become **crazy** heaps of timber.

People were very cautiously coming out to stare at the town. Aruna seemed like a **different**
10 place. It was almost **unrecognizable**.

Sylvie felt **weak**.

2. Adjectives describe things, people, places or ideas.

An adjective, therefore, is always linked to a noun or a pronoun.

Adjectives **modify** nouns and pronouns. To "modify" a word means to add something to the meaning of that word.

In the passage above:

– **safe** (line 1) modifies the pronoun **it**
– **strong** and **old** (line 4) modify the noun **building.**
– **dizzy** (line 5) modifies the pronoun **her.**
– **strange** (line 7) modifies the noun **shapes.**
– **large** (line 7) modifies the noun **trees.**
– **crazy** (line 8) modifies the noun **heaps.**
– **different** (line 10) modifies the noun **place.**
– **unrecognizable** (line 10) modifies the pronoun **it.**
– **weak** (line 11) modifies the noun **Sylvie.**

A3 Practice

1. Put one word in each blank space below.

    If these sentences then make sense, the words you have put in are adjectives.

    Next, identify the noun or pronoun that each adjective modifies.

    A. (a) They live in a _____ village.
       (b) Two _____ children came into the yard.
       (c) We will first have to solve this _____ problem.
       (d) The _____ courthouse was destroyed by fire.
       (e) This has been a very _____ day.

    B. (a) She has gone on a diet because she wants to be _____.
       (b) Dexter's essay was _____ of errors.
       (c) The road ahead seems so _____ that sometimes we feel quite _____.
       (d) It is _____ so hear what they are saying.
       (e) You look _____ in that outfit.

    C. (a) Lead poisoning can make people very _____.
       (b) Young people don't watch that show because they find it _____.
       (c) After several attempts at reviving him, the doctor finally pronounced the man _____.
       (d) The chairperson declared the meeting _____.
       (e) I consider myself _____ to be here.

D. (a) This town is not as _____ as you think.
   (b) The second play was more _____ than the first.
   (c) They plan to hold a competition to determine who is the most _____ farmer.
   (d) Now that the bandits have been caught, the people of the area are less _____.
   (e) The two questions are equally _____.

2. Identify the adjectives in the following sentences, and say what noun or pronoun each adjective modifies.

A. (a) They decided to make a small garden.
   (b) First they cut down the thick bush.
   (c) Then they forked the hard, stony ground.
   (d) It was a difficult task, but they were young, energetic and full of determination.
   (e) The garden was not large, but it was productive.

B. (a) They were having a bitter argument.
   (b) The sink was full of dirty dishes and nobody wanted to wash them.
   (c) Neil said that he had something more important to do.
   (d) Marva said that Neil was just lazy and always wanted to leave the dirty dishes for her.
   (e) When the argument got really loud, Tantie shouted from the yard in an angry voice, and the sink was empty in a flash.

Answers pp. 239-240

Word Classes **A4**

A4 VERBS

1. All the verbs in this passage are in bold type:

Disaster

When she **thought** it **might be** safe, Sylvie **crept** nervously out of the house **to see** the damage. She **could** not **believe** her eyes.

There **was** destruction everywhere. Sylvie suddenly **wanted to run** back into the safety of the strong, old building, but she **checked** herself. She **stood** on the step and **stared** in horror.
5 The sight **made** her dizzy.

The hurricane **had ripped** off the roofs of neighbours' houses. It **had twisted** pieces of metal into strange shapes. It **had torn** up large trees by their roots and **flung** them down again. Some houses **had become** crazy heaps of timber.

People **were** very cautiously **coming** out **to stare** at the town. Aruna **seemed** like a different
10 place. It **was** almost unrecognizable.

Sylvie **felt** weak.

2. Verbs are words which tell of doing or being. They indicate an action or a state.
The "doing" can be physical action, e.g., **crept** (line 1), **to see** (line 1), **had twisted** (line 6), **were coming** (line 9); or it can be mental action, e.g., **thought** (line 1), **believe** (line 2), **wanted** (line 3), **felt** (line 11).

Examples of verbs of being are: **might be** (line 1), **was** (lines 3 and 10), **had become** (line 8), **seemed** (line 9).

A verb takes different forms depending on the work it has to do. These are the features of verb behaviour that you need to know about:

| *The infinitive* | *Auxiliaries* | *Voice* |
| *Participles* | *Tense* | *Mood* |

3. The infinitive

3.1 A verb takes on many forms, but its basic form is the infinitive. This form is the "raw" verb.

Examples of the infinitive in *Disaster* are: **to see** (line 1), **to run** (line 3) **to stare** (line 9).

When we refer to a verb, we use its infinitive form as the official name of the verb. For example, the verbs in the second paragraph of *Disaster* can be identified as follows: **to be** (line 3), **to want** (line 3), **to run** (line 3), **to check** (line 4), **to stand** (line 4), **to stare** (line 4), **to make** (line 5).

3.2 The infinitive is often used without the **to** in front of it. In *Disaster,* **be** (line 1) and **believe** (line 2) are also infinitives. (More on this in E18 and F7).

4. Participles

4.1 The form of the verb which ends with **ing** is known as the **present participle**, e.g., **coming** (line 9).

(More on the present participle in Section H).

4.2 The **past participle** is another form that verbs can take. Most verbs form their past participle by adding **ed** to the infinitive: **ripped** (line 6), **twisted** (line 6).

Others add **t**, **en** or **n**.

Some do not add an ending but change internally, like **flung** (line 7) which comes from **to fling.**

Other verbs do both, for example, **torn** (line 7) which is the past participle of **to tear.**

A few verbs do not change at all: **become** (line 8) is the past participle of **to become.**

(More on the past participle in Section G.)

5. Finite and Non-finite

5.1 In English the infinitive and the participles, when they stand on their own in the sentence, do not do the work of verbs. They act as other parts of speech (see Sections G2 and H1). Most importantly, the present participle acts as a noun and as an adjective, while the past participle acts as an adjective:

Walking keeps you healthy. [Present participle as noun.]

Put on your **walking** shoes. [Present participle as adjective.]

They found the fugitive in an **abandoned** house. [Past participle as adjective.]

5.2 Infinitives and participles are said to be non-finite verbs: unfinished or incomplete verbs. A complete verb is called a **finite verb**.

6. Auxiliaries

6.1 A finite or complete verb may be a single word, for example, in *Disaster:* **thought, crept** (line 1), **was** (lines 3 and 10), **wanted** (line 3), **checked, stood** (line 3), **stared** (line 4), **made** (line 5), **felt** (line 11).

6.2 A finite verb can also be a group of words which we will call a verb phrase. A verb phrase is formed by placing an **auxiliary verb** (or more than one) before an infinitive or a participle.

These are the verb phrases in *Disaster:*

Auxiliary + Infinitive: **might be** (line 1), **could believe** (line 2)

Auxiliary + Past participle: **had ripped** (line 6), **had twisted** (line 6), **had torn** (line 7), **(had) flung, had become** (line 8).

Auxiliary + Present participle: **were coming** (line 9).

6.3 A verb phrase can consist of two, three, or four words, because there can be more than one auxiliary. The last verb is the main verb:

will give

should be giving

would have been given

6.4 Here is a list of auxiliary verbs: **to be, to have, to do, can, could, will, would, shall, should, may, might, must**.

7. Tense

7.1 "Tense" refers to time.

The verb takes on different forms to mark the time of the action or state in relation to the time of speaking.

7.2 There are sixteen tenses in the English language. Eight of these tenses are given here (in bold type):

(a) Ma Charlotte always **walks** to the market. [present simple tense]

(b) Ma Charlotte **walked** to the market last Saturday. [past simple tense]

(c) She **is walking** down the road right at this moment. [present continuous tense]

(d) She **was walking** along Davies Street when it happened. [past continuous tense]

(e) Ma Charlotte **has walked** to the market all her life. [present perfect tense]

(f) They did not know that she **had walked** out of the house. [past perfect tense]

(g) In a little while Ma Charlotte **will walk** through the gate with her basket. [future tense]

(h) She **would have walked** all the way to town if they had let her. [conditional perfect tense]

These tenses are dealt with in different sections of the manual.

8. Voice

"Voice" refers to whether the subject of the verb (B1:2) is **active** or **passive,** and this is reflected in the form of the verb. See G5.

9. Mood

"Mood" refers to the four things a sentence can be used to do:

9.1 The **indicative** is the mood which we use most of the time. It is used for making statements. All the verbs in *Disaster* are in the indicative mood.

9.2 The **interrogative** is the form used for asking questions:

> When **did** Sylvie **creep** out of the house?
>
> **Were** people **coming** out?

9.3 The **imperative** is the form used for giving orders or instructions, or making requests:

> **Come** out of the house.
>
> Please **stand** on the step.

9.4 The **subjunctive** is a somewhat rare form. It can be used to advocate or demand an action; express a wish; or indicate unreality.

See E18:2, F7:5 and F9.

A4 Practice

1. Name the following verbs, i.e., give the infinitive form of each. Remember that when the verb consists of more than one word, the last word is the key one – the "main verb". For example, the infinitive of **had been used** is **to use**.

A. (a) have seen
   (b) did eat
   (c) spoken
   (d) had been caught
   (e) should be announcing

B. (a) decided
   (b) were spinning
   (c) lost
   (d) approaches
   (e) is worn

C. (a) succeeded
   (b) do contain
   (c) will concentrate
   (d) describes
   (e) are attempting

D. (a) chosen
   (b) could have been stealing
   (c) sank
   (d) would have been shaken
   (e) will be flying

2. Identify the verbs in the following sentences:

A. *One-word verbs*
   (a) Today work stopped on that project.
   (b) Government ministries owe large sums of money to the Water and Sewerage Authority.

(c) Sylvester operates a bar on weekends.

(d) The school gave him another chance.

(e) That lady is my sister.

B. *Two-word verbs*

(a) The family is holding a memorial service.

(b) Did you reach any kind of agreement?

(c) In response to the pressure of public opinion, they have submitted another report.

(d) At first nobody would believe her.

(e) We can accommodate three more people.

C. *Three-word verbs*

(a) Your services are being terminated.

(b) By then everyone will have gone home.

(c) The accused has been sent to the mental hospital.

(d) At any moment a new policy may be adopted.

(e) They should have revealed this earlier.

3. See **A1 Practice**. Find the verbs in all the sentences given.

Answers pp. 240-241

A5 ADVERBS

1. Here the words in bold type are adverbs:

Disaster

When she thought it might be safe, Sylvie crept **nervously** out of the house to see the damage. She could **not** believe her eyes.

There was destruction **everywhere**. Sylvie **suddenly** wanted to run **back** into the safety of the strong, old building, but she checked herself. She stood on the step and stared in horror.
5 The sight made her dizzy.

The hurricane had ripped **off** the roofs of neighbours' houses. It had twisted pieces of metal into strange shapes. It had torn **up** large trees by their roots and flung them **down again**. Some houses had become crazy heaps of timber.

People were **very cautiously** coming out to stare at the town. Aruna seemed like a different
10 place. It was **almost** unrecognizable.

Sylvie felt weak.

2. **Just as adjectives work with nouns and pronouns, so adverbs work mainly with verbs, adjectives and other adverbs.**

   An **adverb** is a word which modifies a verb, an adjective or another adverb.
   (Adverbs are to be found in a few other roles, but these are the most important.)

   In *Disaster,* the adverbs work as follows:

   – **nervously** (line 1) modifies the verb **crept**
   – **not** (line 2) modifies the verb **could believe**
   – **everywhere** (line 3) modifies the verb **was**
   – **suddenly** (line 3) modifies the verb **wanted**
   – **back** (line 3) modifies the verb **run**
   – **off** (line 6) modifies the verb **had ripped**
   – **up** (line 7) modifies the verb **torn**
   – **down** and **again** (lines 7-8) modify the verb **had flung**
   – **very** (line 9) modifies the adverb **cautiously**
   – **cautiously** and **out** (line 9) modify the verb **were coming**
   – **almost** (line 10) modifies the adjective **unrecognizable**

3. **Adverbs tell us different things about the words that they modify.**

   Adverbs may tell **how, how much, where, where to, when** or **how often.**

   – **How**: slowly, well, roughly, quickly, helpfully, neatly
   – **How much**: rather, quite, sufficiently, very, almost, somewhat
   – **Where** or **where to**: there, down, upstairs, outside, everywhere, home
   – **When**: yesterday, now, shortly, immediately, then, later
   – **How often**: occasionally, usually, seldom, rarely, frequently, always.

4. **Most adverbs are formed by adding ly to an adjective, but note that**
   – there are many adverbs which do not end with **ly**, and
   – there are many words ending with **ly** which are not adverbs. The following words, for example, are adjectives: **fatherly, leisurely, princely, cowardly.**
   (These words are formed by adding **ly** to a noun.)

5. **Some words can be used as adjective or adverb, for example: straight, fast, next, upstairs, far, overseas, underground.**

6. There are some words, such as off, up, down and out, which sometimes work as adverbs and sometimes as prepositions. (See A6:6.)

7. **Sometimes adverbs do not modify any one word in a sentence.**

   7.1 Adverbs modify modifiers. A modifier can be a phrase (see B6), and so adverbs sometimes modify phrases:

   He felt **completely** out of place.
   They went **straight** down the road.

   7.2 Now and then an adverb "modifies" a whole sentence – it makes a comment on, or gives the speaker's opinion of, what that sentence says:

   Fortunately we got there in time.
   They have rejected the offer, **naturally.**

A5 Practice

Identify the adverbs in the following sentences and say what each modifies.

A. (a) You must write more carefully.
   (b) Your handwriting is almost illegible.
   (c) Some of your letters lean forward, some lean backwards, and some can't make up their minds.
   (d) Sometimes they chase each other crazily across the page.
   (e) Always think about the unfortunate person who has to read what you write.

B. (a) They visit their grandmother regularly.
   (b) Her house is really their second home.
   (c) She is perfectly happy to have them.
   (d) But she is quite strict and never spoils them.
   (e) They rarely misbehave in her house.

C. (a) Yesterday a fair was held in the school.
   (b) The organizers cleaned the place afterwards.
   (c) They worked swiftly and efficiently.
   (d) One group worked upstairs and another downstairs.
   (e) Today the school looks practically new.

Answers p. 242

A6 PREPOSITIONS

1. The words in bold type are prepositions:

Disaster

When she thought it might be safe, Sylvie crept nervously **out of** the house to see the damage. She could not believe her eyes.

There was destruction everywhere. Sylvie suddenly wanted to run back **into** the safety **of** the strong, old building, but she checked herself. She stood **on** the step and stared **in** horror.
5   The sight made her dizzy.

The hurricane had ripped off the roofs **of** neighbours' houses. It had twisted pieces **of** metal **into** strange shapes. It had torn up large trees **by** their roots and flung them down again. Some houses had become crazy heaps **of** timber.

People were very cautiously coming out to stare **at** the town. Aruna seemed **like** a different
10   place. It was almost unrecognizable.

Sylvie felt weak.

2. A preposition usually occurs before a noun or pronoun, creating a prepositional phrase. (See B6:1.)

The preposition is said to "govern" the noun or pronoun. This noun or pronoun is the "object" of the preposition. In line 4, **in** governs **horror,** or, **horror** is the object of **in.**

Determiners (see A9:3.1) and modifiers attached to the noun are part and parcel of a prepositional phrase:

	Preposition	Determiner/Modifier	Object of Preposition
line 4:	of	the strong, old	building
line 6:	of	neighbours'	houses
line 7:	by	their	roots
lines 9-10:	like	a different	place

3. **Prepositional phrases do the same work as adjectives and adverbs: they modify other words.**

   These are the prepositional phrases in *Disaster* and the words they modify:

   - **out of the house** (line 1) modifies **crept**
   - **into the safety** (line 3) modifies **to run**
   - **of the strong, old building** (line 4) modifies **safety**
   - **on the step** (line 4) modifies **stood**
   - **in horror** (lines 4-5) modifies **stared**
   - **of neighbours' houses** (line 6) modifies **roofs**
   - **of metal** (lines 6-7) modifies **pieces**
   - **into strange shapes** (line 7) modifies **twisted**
   - **by their roots** (line 7) modifies **had torn**
   - **of timber** (line 8) modifies **heaps**
   - **at the town** (line 9) modifies **to stare**
   - **like a different place** (line 9-10) modifies **Aruna**

4. **Prepositions can be groups of words, as in line 2: out of.**

5. **Here are only some of the most common prepositions:**

   about, after, along, along with, away from, at, before, behind, by, down, for, from, in, in front of, into, like, near to, next to, of, off, on, out of, over, through, to, under, until, up, upon, up to, with, without.

6. **Some of these words are also used as adverbs. They are adverbs when instead of governing a noun or pronoun, they modify a verb.**

   The following sentence from *Disaster* can help to illustrate this:

   > The hurricane had ripped **off** the roofs of neighbours' houses.

   Here **off** is working with the verb **had ripped,** and not with the noun which follows it – **roofs**. **Off** plays the role of an adverb, modifying **had ripped**.

   In the following sentence its role is different:

   > Water was rolling **off** the roofs of neighbours' houses.

   Here **off** belongs not with the verb **was rolling**, but with the noun **roofs**. It governs **roofs**, and is therefore a preposition in this sentence. The whole phrase **off the roofs of neighbours' houses** is a prepositional phrase that modifies the verb **was rolling**.

A6 Practice

1. Put suitable prepositions in the blank spaces.
   Then underline (or write out) the prepositional phrases you have formed.
   (a) The chain was lost somewhere _____ that big house.
   (b) Beverley was frantically searching _____ it.
   (c) She shone the flashlight _____ the children's wardrobe.
   (d) Her little brother crawled _____ all the beds and looked.
   (e) They eventually found the chain hanging _____ a peg _____ the bathroom.

2. Identify the prepositions in the following sentences. Say what noun each preposition governs. Underline (or write out) the prepositional phrases.

A. (a) They couldn't find the way to the union hall.
   (b) They asked a passerby for directions.
   (c) He told them to go down Grant Street.
   (d) Then at the traffic light they would have to turn left.
   (e) The union hall would be the third building on their right.

B. (a) Mr Richards had about ten cats in his house.
   (b) There was a small calico cat sleeping peacefully on the couch.
   (c) Under the dining-room table a kitten was curled into a ball next to its mother.
   (d) Two more kittens were playing hide-and-seek behind the side-board.
   (e) And perched upon the centre-table, pretending to be an ornament, was a large overfed ginger cat with a collar around its neck.

C. (a) Going into the supermarket with a small child is not such a good idea.
   (b) Vera learned this by bitter experience.
   (c) One Saturday morning she took her three-year-old cousin into Food Fair.
   (d) The child climbed onto counters, pulled things off shelves and ran around the legs of customers.
   (e) In future Vera will leave this child at home when she goes to the supermarket.

3. See **A1 Practice,** Assignment 1.C. All the nouns you have put in are governed by prepositions. Identify these prepositions.

4. See **A2 Practice,** Assignment 2.C. Identify in each sentence a preposition governing a pronoun.

Answers p. 243

A7 CONJUNCTIONS

1. A conjunction is a word which joins words or groups of words:
    (a) Garvin **and** Betty
    (b) poor **but** proud
    (c) now **or** never

    (d) living in an apartment **or** living in a house
    (e) tired from the long trip **yet** ready to start work
    (f) the government of Jamaica **and** the government of Barbados

    (g) He took a taxi **because** he was late
    (h) The rainy season came **so** the plants began to grow
    (i) You must not run into the street **for** that is dangerous.

2. The words in bold type in (a) to (i) are some of the most basic conjunctions. There are many other words which work as conjunctions, such as
    if, until, unless, why, when, that, while, although, since, where.

3. Conjunctions do not only join. They also show a particular relationship between the two things which they join. For example:
    – **or** shows that the two things are alternatives [see (c) and (d) above].
    – **but** shows that the two things are in contrast to each other [see (b) above].
    – **because** shows a cause-and-effect relationship [see (g) above].

4. NB. A conjunction does not always sit between the two things which it joins: the first word of Disaster (p. 19) is a conjunction.

A7 Practice

1. Identify conjunctions in *Disaster* (p. 19).

2. Identify conjunctions in the following sentences.

    (a) Nothing will be done unless you demand action.

    (b) My grandmother is as hefty as a boxer and agile as a cat.

    (c) If it rains heavily you can't drive along that road.

    (d) They get up in the morning and go to that garden come rain or shine.

    (e) Because the two friends were born on the same day, they call themselves twins.

3. Use suitable conjunctions to join these pairs of sentences:

A. (a) She lost her busfare. She had to walk.

   (b) You can go by air. You can go by sea.

   (c) Help yourself to some mangoes. Do not pick any green ones.

   (d) They have everything they need. They are not satisfied.

   (e) The house was demolished. A new one was built.

B. (a) They scrubbed the floor. It was shining clean.

   (b) He was late. He had overslept.

   (c) The driver couldn't understand. The car refused to start.

   (d) The children ran indoors. The bell rang.

   (e) Turn off the TV. Nobody is watching it.

Answers p. 244

A8 INTERJECTIONS

An interjection is a word used to express a strong feeling: surprise, shock, fright, joy, disappointment, pain, anger, etc.

Words such as these are interjections:

Ah! Oh! Ouch! Alas! Damn! Wow!

But almost any word can be used as an interjection:

(a) **No!** We will not allow this.

(b) There are five leaks in the roof – **five!**

(c) **Roti!** We would love some.

A9 WORD CLASSES/WORD SLOTS

1. **We have already seen some cases of words belonging to more than one word class. A word is classified according to the work that it does in a particular sentence.**

For example, words that are normally classified as nouns can also play the role of adjectives:

(a) A **hurricane** is approaching.
(b) We need a **hurricane** lamp.

In sentence (a) **hurricane** is a noun: it names the thing which is approaching.

In sentence (b) **hurricane** modifies **lamp** and therefore has to be seen as an adjective. (See D4 for more on adjectival nouns.)

Here is another example of how a word can play different roles:

(c) They sent the children **outside**.
(d) Rubbish is piling up **outside** our house.
(e) The holiday camp has **outside** toilets.

In sentence (c) **outside** is an adverb: it modifies the verb **sent**.
In (d) **outside** is a preposition: it governs the noun **house**.
In (e) **outside** is an adjective: it modifies the noun **toilets**.

2. **So far we have been putting words into classes by looking at what words do.** Another way of identifying word classes is to look at **where words are**: where in a sentence are you likely to find a noun, a verb, an adjective? Word classes correspond to fixed slots in sentences.

3. Noun slots

3.1 Certain words signal that a noun is coming up:

- **the, a, an** (articles – See C6 and C7)
- quantity words: **some, any, no, many, each, another**
- **this, that, these, those** – when such words are not acting in the place of nouns
- pronouns showing ownership (possessive pronouns): **his, her, their, our, my, its**
- nouns showing ownership (possessive nouns): **the neighbours', Marley's, a girl's**

These words that introduce nouns are called **determiners**. The noun may be the very next word:

> a **place**

Or, modifiers linked to the noun can come between:

> a [different] **place**
> a [completely different] **place**

3.2 Therefore another slot a noun may occupy is after an adjective:

> strange **shapes**

3.3 Nouns are also found after prepositions:

> in **horror**

Again, the noun may or may not be the next word. Between the preposition and the noun you may find determiners (see 3.1 above) and modifiers:

> of [the strong, old] **building**
> in [this woman's humble] **opinion**

In **A1 Practice** 1.C, all the nouns you have put into the blank spaces come after prepositions.

3.4 You will usually find a noun after the expression **there + to be**. The noun may come right after:

> There was **destruction**.

Or determiners and modifiers may fall in between:

> There are [no valid] **reasons**.

3.5 Before a finite verb there is usually a noun – the subject of that verb. (See B1:2.) In **A1 Practice** 1.A all the nouns you have put in are subjects coming before their verbs.

Modifiers may come between subject and verb – not only one-word modifiers but also phrases and clauses. (See B6.)

Less often, the noun that is the subject of a verb comes after that verb. In **A1 Practice** 1.D the nouns to be filled in are subjects coming after their verbs.

3.6 A finite verb may be followed by a noun which is the object or complement of that verb. (See B3-5.) All the blank slots in **A1 Practice** 1.B are for objects of finite verbs.

3.7 A present participle or an infinitive may also have a noun following as its object:

>The person waving the **cutlass** is Benjamin.
>They have come all this way to deliver a **petition**.

4. Pronoun slots

4.1 Pronouns fill some of the same slots as nouns: 3.3, 3.5 and 3.6 above, i.e., after prepositions, and before and after verbs as their subjects, objects or complements.

Most pronouns do not have modifiers coming just before them. Therefore, when a pronoun is an object, it usually comes right after the preposition or verb;

Take a good look at **him**. [Object of preposition]

The street vendors didn't accept **that** so easily. [Object of verb]

Look back at **A2 Practice** 2. The sentences in 2.A have pronouns as their subjects; in 2.B pronouns as objects of verbs: and in 2.C pronouns as objects of prepositions.

4.2 There are two kinds of pronouns showing ownership (possessive pronouns):

4.2.1 One kind goes before nouns: see **Noun slots** 3.1. These are sometimes classified as adjectives. In **A2 Practice** 2.D all the pronouns are of this type.

4.2.2 The other kind – e.g., **mine, yours, hers, theirs** – fills noun slots 3.3, 3.5 and 3.6:

What are you going to do with **yours**? [After preposition]

Mine has fallen apart. [Subject of verb]

She threw **hers** away. [Object of verb]

All of this land is **theirs**. [Complement]

5. Adjective slots

5.1 An adjective may come right before the noun which it modifies: **large** trees; **crazy** heaps. In **A3 Practice** 1.A each adjective you have put in comes right before a noun. A whole list of adjectives might precede a noun:

>the **strong, old** building;
>**fat, lazy, greedy** dogs.

5.2 Often the verb **to be** leads to an adjective:

>These bananas are **green**.

Words modifying the adjective may come in between:

>It was [almost] **unrecognizable**.

In A3 Practice 1.B this adjective slot is shown in sentences (a), (b) and (d). (See also B.5:1.)

5.3 In the sentence pattern **The sight made her dizzy**, the adjective **dizzy** comes after the word which it modifies. That word – the pronoun **her** – is the object of the verb. An adjective can come after a noun or a pronoun in this position:

>Teachers call that boy **brilliant**.

This is the adjective slot shown in **A3 Practice** 1.C. It is known as an object complement. (See also B5:2.)

5.4 Adjectives are sometimes introduced by words which show comparison: **more, most, less, least, as, equally**. See **A3 Practice** 1.D.

6. Verb slots

6.1 A verb usually comes after its subject, which can be a noun or a pronoun: Sylvie **crept**. It **had twisted**.

Subject and verb, however, are not always so close together. Moreover, the verb sometimes goes before its subject. See **Noun slots** 3.5.

6.2 Verbs are often coupled with adverbs. The verb may sit before or after the adverb that modifies it:

>Sylvie **crept** nervously. . .
>Sylvie suddenly **wanted**. . .

>See **Adverb slots** 7.1.

7. Adverb slots

7.1 Where there's a verb, there's likely to be an adverb modifying it. This adverb (or these adverbs) may sit

- before the verb: They **often** visit us.
- after the verb: It had torn **up** large trees.
- in the middle of the verb: when the verb is a group of words, adverbs can come between the auxiliary (or the first auxiliary) and the rest of the verb:

    People were **very cautiously** coming out.

    The house should **never** have been sold.

    But an adverb is not always so near to its verb:

    Eventually the members of the team came to accept their defeat.

    They gathered up their belongings **reluctantly**.

7.2 Adverbs usually come before the adjectives that they modify: **almost** unrecognizable; **deliberately** rude.

7.3 Adverbs may come in pairs, the first one modifying the second: **very cautiously; rather boldly**.

7.4 Adverbs may open or close a sentence. See the last two examples in 7.1 above.

7.5 An adverb often opens or closes the sentence when it is not linked to any one word in the sentence but makes a comment on the whole statement. (See A5:7.2.) Such an adverb may also be spliced in somewhere in the sentence:

Typically, Nnamdi has left the kitchen in a mess.

Nnamdi has left the kitchen in a mess – **typically**.

Nnamdi, **typically**, has left the kitchen in a mess.

8. Preposition slots

Prepositions come before nouns and pronouns. See **Noun slots** 3.3 and **Pronoun slots** 4.1.

9. Conjunction slots

9.1 A conjunction falls between two words, phrases or clauses that it joins together. See A7.

9.2 Some conjunctions which join clauses can go before the first clause instead of between the two:

Because he was late, he lost a valuable opportunity.

While they went about their business, plans were quietly being laid.

9.3 A conjunction appears between the last two items on a list:

Port-of-Spain, Kingston, Bridgetown, Castries **and** St George's are capitals of Caribbean countries.

I don't care whether you put it under the house, leave it at the side of the road, throw it in the dustbin **or** burn it.

10. Interjection slots

Like the adverb which expresses the speaker's feelings on the content of a sentence, an interjection usually opens or closes the sentence:

Wow! Look at that rain!
They've used up all the butter, **dammit!**

B. The Sentence

B1 WHAT IS A SENTENCE?

1. People take words and put them together into sentences to express ideas.

However, not just any group of words is a sentence. Look at these:

(a) my grandmother's first daughter

(b) six metres long

(c) won the calypso competition

(d) under the house

None of these really tells us enough.

(a) refers to a person, but what about her?

What, in (b), is six metres long?

Who won the calypso competition?

What is happening under the house?

Each of these word-groups is only a piece of a sentence. None of them expresses a whole idea.

The following groups of words are sentences:

My grandmother's first daughter started a school in the village.

Their platform will be six metres long.

The Mighty Calamity has won the calypso competition again this year.

At night the animals sleep under the house.

2. Subject and verb

To be an English sentence, a group of words must have two basic members: there must be a **subject,** and that subject must have a **verb**.

Let us look again at the sentences above. Each sentence is made up of many words, but we will pick out only the subject and verb of each.

One line is drawn under the subject and two lines under the verb:

My grandmother's first <u>daughter started</u> a school in the village.

Their <u>platform will be</u> six metres long.

<u>The Mighty Calamity has won</u> the calypso competition again this year.

At night the <u>animals sleep</u> under the house.

The subject identifies persons or things.

The verb indicates an action or state, and the subject refers to who or what performs that action or experiences that state.

3. Finite verb

The verbs underlined are all **finite**. (See A4:5 and 6.)

To be a sentence, a group of words must contain a subject and a **finite verb**.

Therefore, the following are not sentences, even though they contain verb forms:

   (e) the person driving the tractor

   (f) the best way to tackle this

   (g) prizes given to the best students

The "verbs" in these groups of words are not finite.

   Driving in (e) is a participle

   To tackle in (f) is an infinitive

   Given in (g) is a participle

4. Expanded sentences

A sentence may look like this:

(a) While neighbours are very concerned about the conditions under which these children are living, they are reluctant to intervene or even to alert the authorities, because they fear that they might be accused of meddling in the family's affairs, and that this might create tensions which they are unable to handle.

Or, a sentence may look like this:

(b) Neighbours intervened.

Sentence (a) contains several subjects and finite verbs. It is made up of a number of clauses. (See B6.)

Sentence (b) has one subject and one finite verb. A sentence with only one subject and one verb can also be quite long:

(c) After many months of watching and waiting, agonizing over the problem, feeling guilty, feeling sorry, turning a blind eye and hoping for somebody else to act, some neighbours finally intervened to bring to an end this shameful situation of child abuse in their midst.

Sentence (c) really boils right down to sentence (b):

Subject: **neighbours**. Verb: **intervened**.

The rest of sentence (c) consists of modifying words and phrases.

5. **The basic sentence**

Some sentences also have an object, and some have a complement. Every sentence boils down to one of the following basic patterns, or more than one of these joined together into one unit:

1. A SUBJECT and A VERB

2. A SUBJECT and A VERB and AN OBJECT

3. A SUBJECT and A VERB and A COMPLEMENT

B2 THE SUBJECT

Subjects can be (1) single words, (2) phrases or (3) clauses.

1. **Single-word subject**

    1.1 The word that is the subject is a noun or a pronoun.

    > **Cars** are approaching at high speed.
    >
    > **She** has passed the exam.

    Remember that the present participle can behave like a noun (see A4:4.1 and 5.1, and H1):

    > **Repainting** is out of the question.

    1.2 A subject can be a list of single words:

    > **Cars, trucks and buses** are approaching.

2. Phrase as subject

2.1 The subject word may be part of a group of words – a noun phrase:

The temperature in this room has dropped slightly.

Some very sleek and expensive-looking cars are approaching at high speed.

Repainting a house of this size is out of the question.

2.2 Phrases can also come in lists:

The smoking of cigarettes, the consumption of alcohol and **the lack of exercise** have contributed to his poor condition.

2.3 **BEWARE!**

A prepositional phrase (see A6) **cannot** be the subject of a sentence. This is incorrect:

X *<u>By forming consumer cooperatives</u>* will help to lower prices.

Prepositional phrases can only be modifiers, i.e., they can only fill adjective or adverb slots. They cannot fill noun slots.

(This and other errors of sentence construction will be discussed in more detail in Level 2 of this manual.)

A correct form of the sentence above is:

Forming consumer cooperatives will help to lower prices.

3. Clause as subject

See **What is a clause?** B6:2.

This sentence has a clause as its subject:

How you express your views makes a difference.

The subject of this sentence is a list of clauses:

In some situations **what you say, when you say it,** and **how you say it** are all equally important.

B2 Practice

In the sentences below, identify finite verbs and their subjects. (Remember that within a sentence there can be more than one subject and verb.)

Where the subject is a group of words, pick out from among them the noun or pronoun that is the subject word.

A. (a) We assembled at the foot of the hill.
   (b) Grace is talking to herself again.
   (c) Aruna seemed like a different place.
   (d) All of our members live in LaGrange or in communities nearby.
   (e) Their chickens are roaming all over the place.

B. (a) It was a difficult task, but they were young, energetic and full of determination.
   (b) When the argument got really loud, Tantie shouted from the yard in an angry voice, and the sink was empty in a flash.
   (c) Today work stopped on that project.
   (d) Going into the supermarket with a small child is not such a good idea.
   (e) By then everyone will have gone home.

C. (a) She stood on the step.
   (b) If it rains heavily you can't drive along that road.
   (c) They rarely misbehave.
   (d) One group worked upstairs and another downstairs.
   (e) Today the school looks practically new.

Answers p. 244

B3 THE OBJECT

1. (a) The bus hit a pedestrian.
   (b) She has passed the exam.
   (c) The Quaminas are building a house.
   (d) Trinidad and Tobago exports oil.
   (e) Privileges bring responsibility.

Each of these sentences has three important parts:

There is a person or thing performing an action – the **subject**.

There is the action – the **verb**.

And the action has a target – the **object**.

Subject	Verb	Object
The bus	hit	a pedestrian
She	has passed	the exam
The Quaminas	are building	a house
Trinidad and Tobago	exports	oil
Privileges	bring	responsibility

The **subject** tells us who or what performs the action.

The **verb** tells us what the action is.

The **object** tells us whom or what the verb acts upon: what is the target of the action.

The bus hit **whom**? A pedestrian.

She has passed **what?** The exam.

The Quaminas are building **what?** A house.

Trinidad and Tobago exports **what?** Oil.

Privileges bring **what?** Responsibility.

The object answers the question **whom?** or **what?** after the verb.

2. **In the following sentences the verb does not act upon anything, so there is no object.**

(a) They are eating upstairs.

(b) The children sang with great energy.

(c) Work begins at eight o'clock.

Subjects and verbs are underlined. So what about the words that come after the verbs? Are they objects?

They are **not** objects, because they do not tell us what the verb acts upon.

(a) They are eating **what?** Does "upstairs" answer this question? Is "upstairs" a kind of food that they are eating? No. "Upstairs" simply tells us **where** the eating is taking place, not **what** is being eaten.

(b) The children sang **what?** Is "with great energy" the name of the song that they were singing? No. This part of the sentence does not tell us **what** they were singing, but **how** they were singing.

(c) Does "work" begin anything? No. "At eight o'clock" tells us **when** work begins, not **what**.

The extra words just tell us something about the verb: they are modifiers. They modify the verb. (See **ADVERBS** and B6:4, **Roles of phrases and clauses**.)

3. **An object is not just anything that comes after the verb.**

    The object answers the question **whom** or **what** does the verb act upon, not where, or how, or when.

    Objects of verbs, like subjects, are nouns, pronouns, noun phrases or noun clauses.

4. **There are some verbs which cannot have an object. Some examples of these are: to sleep, to laugh, to go, to come, to stroll, to lie.**

    You cannot sleep something or somebody, nor can you laugh something or somebody:

    X *I slept my bed.*
    X *He laughed his sister when she fell down.*

    Try to give an object to any of the other verbs on the list above, and you will realize that you are producing nonsense. Verbs like these are known as **intransitive** verbs.

    Verbs which can have an object are called **transitive** verbs.

5. The objects we have looked at in B3 are **direct objects.** In the next section we look at indirect objects.

B3 Practice

Some of the sentences below have objects. Some do not. Identify the subject and verb of each sentence, and the object where there is one.

If the object is a group of words, pick out from among them the noun or pronoun that is the object word.

A. (a) The police arrested two suspects.

(b) They appeared in court on Wednesday.

(c) Trevor and Naima entered the race this year.

(d) They trained for months before the day.

(e) Our panside celebrates its tenth anniversary next week.

B. (a) Ma Charlotte walked to the market last Saturday.

(b) That embarrassed him.

(c) First they cut down the thick bush.

(d) Then they forked the hard, stony ground.

(e) You must write more carefully.

C. (a) They visit their grandmother regularly.

(b) Sylvie crept nervously out of the house.

(c) The organizers cleaned the place afterwards.

(d) Mr Richards had about ten cats in his house.

(e) One Saturday morning she took her three-year-old cousin into Food Fair.

Answers p. 245

B4 THE INDIRECT OBJECT

1. (a) A community organization has sent the firm a letter of protest.

    (b) The meeting gave Learie a round of applause.

    (c) The graduating class bought their teacher a farewell present.

    (d) They will have to find us a new site.

    Each of these sentences has two objects – two different kinds of objects.

    The word underlined twice is a **direct** object, discussed in B3. This is the more regular kind of object.

    The word with one line under it is an **indirect object.**

2. The indirect object is a person or thing that gets something out of the action of the verb.

    An indirect object generally goes with a direct object:

The direct object answers the question whom/what after the verb, while the indirect object answers the question to whom/what, or for whom/what.

3. **The indirect object can be replaced by a prepositional phrase introduced by to or for.**
   The sentences (a) to (d) above can therefore be rewritten as follows:

   (a) A community organization has sent a letter of protest **to the firm**.

   (b) The meeting gave a round of applause **to Learie**.

   (c) The graduating class bought a farewell present **for their teacher**.

   (d) They will have to find a new site **for us**.

B4 Practice

Identify the direct and indirect objects in the following sentences.

A. (a) When we grow up we will build our grandparents a new house.

   (b) She was so shaken that somebody poured her a drink of brandy.

   (c) They don't teach children manners any more.

   (d) Can you spare me a moment, please?

   (e) The air hostess served passengers breakfast in the middle of the night.

B. (a) The police officer read Craig the warrant on the spot.

   (b) People are renting students substandard accommodation at exorbitant rates.

   (c) The debating team has secured the school a place in the finals.

   (d) Christine told Laila all her secrets.

   (e) They made themselves some cheese sandwiches.

Answers p. 245

B5 THE COMPLEMENT

1. Subject complements

1.1 (a) This <u>is</u> <u>it</u>.

   (b) Ma <u>remains</u> the <u>boss</u>.

   (c) Their future <u>seemed</u> <u>grim</u>.

   (d) The milk <u>tasted</u> <u>sour</u>.

   (e) Trevor <u>was getting</u> <u>fat</u>.

   (f) Margaret <u>will become</u> an <u>accountant</u>.

   (g) Somebody <u>has gone</u> <u>crazy</u>.

   These sentences are made up of a subject, a **linking verb** and a **complement.** The verb is underlined once, the complement twice.

1.2 Look at the relationship between the subject and the complement.

   The complement is either

   – a **noun** or **pronoun** which refers to the same person or thing that is the subject,

   OR

   – an **adjective** which describes the subject.

   The linking verb, therefore, is like an equal sign in mathematics: the two things on either side of it are the same.

This	=	it
Ma	=	boss
future	=	grim
milk	=	sour

   In these sentences the complement is a term which can be said to "mirror" the subject. This part of the sentence is known as the subject complement.

   Subject and subject complement are connected to each other by a **linking verb**.

1.3 The subject complement is a noun, pronoun or adjective slot. It can be filled by single words as well as by phrases or clauses:

Their future seemed **grimmer than ever.**

This is **what we want.**

1.4 Linking verbs are verbs which tell of being, seeming or becoming. The following are the most commonly used linking verbs:

Being/seeming
to be, to remain, to stay, to taste, to smell, to sound, to feel, to seem, to appear, to look.

Becoming
to become, to grow, to get, to go, to turn.

1.5 Linking verbs are **intransitive**. (See B3:4.)

Note, however, that some of these verbs can also be used transitively. That is, they can have an object instead of a complement.

When they have an object, i.e., when they are transitive, they are not linking verbs.

(a) At the sound of the bell the class grew **silent**.

(b) This term the class grew **cucumbers** in their garden.

In (a) **silent** is a complement, but in (b) **cucumbers** is an object. We cannot say **class = cucumbers**.

1.6 If these verbs are followed by words which do not "mirror" the subject, then those words are not complements.

Trevor remained **upstairs**.

This child is growing **by leaps and bounds**.

The portion in bold type in each of these two sentences modifies the verb. These are not complements.

2. Object complements

In the sections above we looked at subject complements.

2.1 With certain verbs a direct object may also have a complement. In each of the following sentences the part in bold type is an **object complement**:

(a) The sight made her **dizzy**.

(b) Some children find that film **boring**.

(c) The Public Health authorities have declared the premises **unfit for human habitation.**

(d) We do not consider them **criminals**.

(e) Our women's group has elected Wilma **Public Relations Officer.**

(f) They will name their baby **whatever they choose**.

These sentences follow the basic pattern SUBJECT-VERB-DIRECT OBJECT, and the object is complemented (or completed) by a word or group of words coming after it.

2.2 An object complement, like a subject complement, may be either a noun or an adjective (or equivalent group of words).

In sentences (a) to (c) above, the object complement is either an adjective or an adjective phrase.

In (d) to (f) the complements are, respectively, a noun, a noun phrase and a noun clause.

2.3 Identify the direct objects.

The direct object comes just before its complement:

(a) her   (b) film   (c) premises   (d) them   (e) Wilma   (f) baby

2.4 It is verbs such as the following which may have an object with a complement:

to call, to consider, to declare, to deem, to dub, to elect, to find, to leave, to make, to name, to pronounce, to render, to strike.

B5 Practice

1. Some of these sentences follow the pattern SUBJECT-VERB-COMPLEMENT. Pick out those which do. Identify the subject, the verb and the subject complement of each. Where the subject or subject complement is a word that is part of a phrase, identify the word.

A. (a) Sylvie felt weak.
   (b) The doctor is sounding the patient's heart.
   (c) His latest calypso sounds really good.
   (d) Sarah was the youngest child.
   (e) We can't stay in this place forever.

B. (a) They appeared in court on Wednesday.

(b) Some houses had become crazy heaps of timber.

(c) After the fête, the job of cleaning up will be yours.

(d) This dog looks quite fierce.

(e) By now everybody was looking at Harry.

C. (a) The fish in the pot has gone bad already.

(b) The proposed demolition of those houses is becoming a really controversial issue.

(c) My son has turned Catholic.

(d) The motorcade has just turned the corner.

(e) One question we still have not answered is why did this happen?

2. Identify the object and object complement in each of the following sentences:

(a) We consider this a breach of promise.

(b) He always leaves the place clean.

(c) Everybody called her "Mother".

(d) Your action has rendered our contract null and void.

(e) God strike me dead if I'm lying.

Answers p. 246

B6 PHRASES AND CLAUSES

1. **What is a phrase?**

    1.1 (a) the development of our country

    (b) children taken out of school

    (c) a woman driving a car

    (d) to make uniforms compulsory

    (e) in certain cases

    (f) eating in restaurants

    The word-groups above are all phrases.

    1.2 The difference between a phrase and a sentence is that a phrase does not contain a subject with a finite verb. (See A4:5.)

1.3 Whereas a sentence makes complete sense, a phrase does not. This does not mean, however, that a phrase makes no sense at all. A phrase is not just any old collection of words without subject and finite verb:

> country development the our of
> out school children of taken

These are not phrases, at least not in English.

A phrase does not make complete sense on its own, but it does make some sense. For it to make sense, it must follow a recognizable pattern, just as sentences must follow recognizable sentence patterns.

1.4 There are several different phrase patterns in English, but we need not describe them all here. The reason why we can tell the difference between a scrambled collection of words and an English phrase is that unconsciously we know the patterns.

Let us look at one of the phrases given above. Phrase (a) consists of a noun followed by a prepositional phrase. These two parts form a unit because they are related to each other: the prepositional phrase modifies the noun. We can create other phrases on this same pattern:

> a taste of our Carnival
> the launching of this project
> his idea of a party
> those houses by the river
> the people with no money
> our place in the sun

The pattern is

Determiner + Noun followed by **Preposition + Determiner + Noun**

2. What is a clause?

2.1 A clause *does* contain a finite verb with a subject.

A sentence is a clause.

Not every clause, however, is a sentence.

2.2 There are two kinds of clauses – independent and subordinate.

A sentence is an **independent clause**. It can stand on its own and make complete sense.

Other clauses are **dependent** or **subordinate**. They cannot stand on their own.

The following are independent clauses, or sentences:

    (a) We heard the news.

    (b) Nobody was there.

    (c) Agriculture is very important.

The following are subordinate clauses:

    (d) when we heard the news

    (e) because nobody was there

    (f) which is very important

3. Subordinators

If all clauses have a subject and finite verb, how do we tell independent clauses from subordinate clauses?

A subordinate clause begins with a **subordinator**. In the clauses (d) - (f) the subordinators are **when**, **because** and **which**.

Subordinate clauses cannot stand on their own. They have to be attached to an independent clause. A subordinator is like a chain placed on a clause to make you attach it to a sentence. Subordinators are words which take away the independence of a clause.

Here are some of the most common subordinators:

when	though	where	what
whenever	although	how	whatever
before	if	why	whether
after	as	when	unless
since	as if	who	because
while	in order that	whoever	which
until	so that	that	whichever

Note that some subordinators are single words, and some are groups of words.

4. Roles of phrases and clauses

Phrases and clauses act as modifiers (i.e., adjectives and adverbs), and as nouns.

4.1 In the following three sentences, the same noun is modified by (a) an adjective, (b) an adjectival phrase, and (c) an adjectival clause:

   (a) They had to make a **crucial** decision.

   (b) They had to make a decision **about their future.**

   (c) They had to make a decision **that would change their lives forever.**

4.2 In the three sentences below, the same verb is modified by (a) an adverb, (b) an adverbial phrase, and (c) an adverbial clause:

   (a) Incidents like these must be reported **immediately.**

   (b) Incidents like these must be reported **without a moment's delay.**

   (c) Incidents like these must be reported **as soon as they occur.**

4.3 In the sentences below, the subject slot is filled by (a) a noun, (b) a noun phrase, and (c) a noun clause:

   (a) **Restaurants** can sometimes be unhealthy.

   (b) **Eating in restaurants** can sometimes be unhealthy.

   (c) **What they serve in restaurants** can sometimes be unhealthy.

5. Main clause

A phrase or a subordinate clause is only **part** of a sentence. A phrase or a subordinate clause must be attached to an independent clause.

The independent clause in a sentence is called the **main clause.** (There can be more than one main clause in a sentence.)

In the following sentences, main clauses are in bold type. Only the core of each main clause is identified – (a) subject + verb; (b) subject + verb + complement; (c) subject + verb + object:

(a) When the argument got really loud, **Tantie shouted** from the yard in an angry voice.

(b) While neighbours are very concerned about the conditions under which these children are living, **they are reluctant** to intervene or even to alert the authorities, because they feel that they might be accused of meddling in the family's affairs, and that this might create tensions which they are unable to handle.

(c) If it rains heavily **you can't drive your car** along that road.

6. Punctuation

Begin a sentence with a capital letter, and at the end of the sentence put a full stop.

When a sentence consists of more than one clause, the whole group of words is punctuated as one sentence. There is a capital letter at the beginning of the first clause, and the full stop does not come until the end of the last clause. See 5. above: sentences (a) – (c).

Do **not** put a capital letter at the beginning and a full stop at the end of a group of words which is not a sentence.

Phrases and subordinate clauses are not sentences. To punctuate a non-sentence as though it were a sentence is an error.

A non-sentence punctuated as a sentence is called a **sentence fragment**.

(More on sentence fragments and other errors of sentence construction in Level 2 of this manual.)

B6 Practice

1. Indicate which of the following are phrases, which are subordinate clauses, and which are sentences:

A. (a) what we have seen developing over the past few months
   (b) also on the agenda for the meeting
   (c) the secretary resigned
   (d) the political crisis has come to an end
   (e) although the board has given its approval

B. (a) the young people involved in this programme
   (b) after the exhibition was set up
   (c) to settle outstanding bills

(d) the street vendors of the capital city have formed an association
(e) more and more people are developing the habit of saving

C. (a) many species of wildlife are facing extinction
(b) until all the old stock has been sold
(c) when the aircraft stopped at the end of the runway
(d) entrusted with the safety of the nation
(e) when the fire was finally brought under control, looters took over the building

2. Identify the main clauses in the following sentences – subject, verb, object if there is one, complement if there is one:

A. (a) As the hurricane season approaches, it is essential that we make certain preparations.
(b) She would have walked all the way to town if they had let her.
(c) Professor Chung began his lecture at the scheduled time even though there were only three students in the auditorium.
(d) The garden was not large, but it was productive.
(e) Because the two friends were born on the same day, they call themselves twins.

B. (a) When we grow up we will build our grandparents a new house.
(b) They became very fit, and both were able to run the whole distance.
(c) Nothing will be done unless you demand action.
(d) Whenever that dog hears a vehicle approaching, it rushes out into the road.
(e) Traffic was diverted in order that the march might proceed unobstructed.

3. Divide the following passages into sentences by putting capital letters and full stops where they belong:

A. if you write illegibly in an exam then you have failed before you even start the examiners are not going to waste time trying to decipher what you have written when they might have hundreds of other papers to mark bad handwriting is bad manners it shows a lack of consideration for those who have to read what you write

B. about three years ago a new law was passed making it an offence to litter streets and other public places people ignored it at first and continued to treat the whole country as one large dustbin driving along the highways they threw beer bottles and cigarette boxes out of cars in the towns and villages streets were still strewn with every kind of rubbish casually dropped by pedestrians or piled on the pavement by businesspeople a river was a place where you could throw anything from a dead dog to a derelict motor car after about a week the police actually started to prosecute people for littering the offenders were quite indignant they thought it was perfectly in order to fling away things that they didn't need any longer it was a clear case of the government violating people's human rights the courts slapped some heavy fines on those found guilty of littering and people soon began to appreciate the human right of all citizens to live in a clean environment.

Answers pp. 246-247

Noun Forms

C. Number

C1 SINGULAR AND PLURAL

Nouns and pronouns can refer to either one thing or person, or more than one. Here we will concentrate on nouns.

When a noun refers to **one** thing or person, we say that it is **singular** in number.

When a noun refers to **more than one** thing or person, we say that it is **plural** in number.

In English the normal way of showing that a noun is plural is to put an **s** on the end of it:

   singular: year   **plural:** years

The **s** ending is a plural **marker**.

When the noun stands bare (without an **s** added to it), the noun is singular – usually. In C3 we look at exceptions.

C1 Practice

Identify singular and plural nouns in the following sentences:

A. (a) We assembled at the foot of the hill.
   (b) After three days she still had not returned.
   (c) The photographer took a picture of that for the records.
   (d) Their chickens are roaming all over the place.
   (e) New locks were installed at his request.

B. (a) The sink was full of dirty dishes and nobody wanted to wash them.
   (b) In response to the pressure of public opinion, they have submitted another report.
   (c) The child climbed onto counters, pulled things off shelves and ran around the legs of customers.
   (d) And perched upon the centre-table, pretending to be an ornament, was a large overfed ginger cat with a collar around its neck.
   (e) There will be food, drinks, games, and above all, music.

C. (a) When we grow up we will build our grandparents a new house.
   (b) Whenever that dog hears a vehicle approaching, it rushes out into the road.

(c) She was so shaken that somebody poured her a drink of brandy.

(d) His latest calypso sounds really good.

(e) The proposed demolition of these houses is becoming a really controversial issue.

Answers pp. 247-248

C2 DIFFERENT WAYS OF ADDING S

1. **For most English nouns you simply add an s to make the plural.** This is not so for all nouns, however.

    Study the following patterns in order to avoid spelling problems.

2. **Words ending with sh, ch, x, s**

    Look at these words:

    bush, church, tax, bus.

    Try simply adding an **s** to each. How will you now pronounce the word?

    You can't – it's too awkward. You need another sound in between:

    bush**es**, church**es**, tax**es**, bus**es**.

    How will you know when to add **es**?

    You add **es** for the plural if the noun ends with any of these: **sh, ch, x, s.**

wish	ditch	box	thermos
brush	coach	reflex	kiss
lash	bench	hoax	chorus
leash	clutch	sex	business
dish	porch	fox	mass

    On the other hand, do not add **es** when you don't have to. These are wrong:

    X *clockes, numberes, wordes.*

3. **Words ending with o**

    3.1 You also put **es** onto most words which end with **o**:

    | mango | – | mango**es** |
    | potato | – | potato**es** |
    | hero | – | hero**es** |

3.2 But there are others to which you simply add the **s**:

    piano – pianos   pimento - pimentos
    photo – photos   radio - radios

When in doubt, use the dictionary.

4. Words ending with y

When words end with **y** and you have to add an **s**, be on your guard.

4.1 If there is a **vowel** (a, e, i, o, u) right before the **y**, then there is no problem. You simply add the **s**:

    bay   –   bays
    monkey   –   monkeys
    toy   –   toys
    guy   –   guys

4.2 But if the letter before the **y** is a consonant, then you have to do something different. (All the letters except a, e, i, o, u are consonants.)

*When the **y** follows a consonant, this **y** is a separate syllable.*

Look at these words:

    baby   –   bab**ies**
    study   –   stud**ies**
    country   –   countr**ies**
    uncertainty   –   uncertaint**ies**
    spy   –   sp**ies**

What has happened here?

First we changed the **y** at the end of the word into an **i**.

Then we added **es**.

4.3 Practise with these nouns. Take off the **y** and add **ies** to make them plural:

    gallery   lady
    enemy   gully
    dolly   nursery
    twenty   fly
    difficulty   story

4.4 Then make these plural:

    joy   alley
    way   decoy
    donkey   pulley
    buoy   holiday
    tray   storey

5. Words ending with f, fe

5.1 In some (not all) words ending with **f** or **fe**, you have to change the **f** to **v** to make the plural ending.
In these words the plural ending is **ves**:

knife	–	knives	calf	–	calves	shelf	–	shelves
wife	–	wives	half	–	halves	loaf	–	loaves
life	–	lives	self	–	selves	thief	–	thieves

5.2 BUT: roofs, beliefs, safes, puffs

When in doubt, use the dictionary.

C2 Practice

Write out the plural forms of the following nouns:

(a) decoy, match, possibility, leaf, beach

(b) stitch, dictionary, chief, dish, party

(c) highway, wharf, company, fax, family

(d) holiday, loss, assembly, scarf, class

(e) cliff, patch, attorney, wolf, copy.

Answers p. 248

C3 OTHER PLURAL FORMS

1. **Some nouns follow different rules, adding neither s nor es for the plural.** Some nouns have a different plural marker, and some have no plural marker at all.

2. **Words from Latin and Greek**

   Some nouns which come from Latin and Greek change their endings as in Latin and Greek:

criterion	–	criteria	crisis	–	crises
medium	–	media	index	–	indices
stimulus	–	stimuli	alumna	–	alumnae

   2.1 Some words like these have two plurals. For example the plural of **medium** can be either **media** or **mediums**.

   2.2 Some foreign words have regular English plurals only, e.g., **virus - viruses**.

   When in doubt, use the dictionary.

3. Plural ending en

A few nouns add **en** for the plural:

ox	–	oxen
child	–	children

4. Internal change

In some nouns the plural is not shown by an ending. Instead, a change takes place inside the word:

tooth	–	teeth
foot	–	feet
man	–	men
woman	–	women
mouse	–	mice

5. No change

A few others remain the same whether singular or plural.

deer	–	deer
sheep	–	sheep
species	–	species

6. No singular

People, **police** and **cattle** are some commonly used nouns which are plural but have no **s** ending and no singular form.

For the singular of **people** we have to use **person**, **man**, **woman** or **child**.

For the singular of **police** we use **police officer**, **policeman** or **policewoman**.

For the singular of **cattle** we must name the individual animal: **cow, bull, heifer**, etc.

NB: When the word **people** means "nation" or "race", it is singular, and its plural form is **peoples:**

The peoples of the world.

C3 Practice

In the lists given below, turn all singular nouns into the plural, and all plural nouns into the singular. *Beware!* Some of these nouns have regular plurals, some have irregular plurals and some have two plurals. You will need to use the dictionary.

(a) campus, synopsis, phenomena, focus, geese

(b) memorandum, people, basis, cactus, formulae

(c) stadium, analyses, metamorphosis, curricula, chorus

(d) larvae, nucleus, syllabus, symposia, appendix

(e) lice, hypothesis, electron, fishermen, antenna

Answers p. 248

The Knots In English

C4 PLURAL MARKERS: CREOLE V. ENGLISH

1. **Different languages show number in different ways.** In English the most common plural marker is an **s** ending. Creole shows plural in a different way.

2. ***CREOLE GRAMMAR***

> A. (a) She gone to feed the **pig** and them.
> (b) Those market **vendor** thiefing people.
> (c) He say them **chair** too low.
> (d) The **man** them go on bad.
>
> B. (a) It have plenty **chennette** on the ground.
> (b) Bring some **bench** from upstairs.
> (c) Miss Ruby have five **pickney**.
>
> All of the nouns underlined here refer to more than one item, but they look the same as the singular.
>
> 2.1. In batch A, certain markers have been used to show more than one: **and them, those, them**. These are the Creole plural markers.
>
> 2.2. In batch B we know that the underlined nouns are plural because each of them is introduced by a quantity word indicating plural: **plenty, some, five**. For Creole speakers this is enough. We do not feel the need to put in another plural marker.

3. We have seen that in English a change is made on the noun word to show that it is plural. In Creole nothing happens to the word itself: a noun remains the same, whatever its number, because the plural marker is separate from the word.

This is one of the reasons why Creole speakers sometimes leave plural nouns unchanged in English. They do this especially when there are other words in the sentence (quantity expressions) which show that the noun refers to more than one:

X (a) *They are offering ten scholarship.*

X (b) *Those student do not like to read.*

X (c) *I do not like these advertisement*

X (d) *She is sending Christmas cards to all of her friend.*

X (e) *There are many restaurant in this town.*

The writers of these sentences have carried Creole grammar over into English. The underlined words are plural nouns, but they have no **s** ending, as in Creole. Each of these nouns has a word or phrase introducing it which suggests "plural" – a plural **marker**:

(a) ten
(b) those
(c) these
(d) all of
(e) many

The writers, therefore, did not bother to change the form of the noun word.

In English you still have to put the plural ending on the noun, even when there is a plural marker by it.

In English a plural noun without a plural ending is an error – with a few exceptions (C3:4-6).

C4 Practice

1. In the five sentences given above, change the underlined nouns into the plural. First say each corrected sentence aloud, and then write it down.

2. Take each of the same sentences in turn and put different plural nouns in place of the ringed one. For example:
   (a) They are offering ten_____.
   They are offering ten books.
   They are offering ten tickets.
   They are offering ten prizes.
   Find at least five new nouns for each sentence.
   Say each of your new sentences aloud before writing it down.

3. In each of the following sentences there is an error – a singular noun that must be made plural. Find the error and correct it:
   (a) *People scattered in all direction when the bomb went off.*
   (b) *There are two distinct season in this country.*
   (c) *These new techniques have raised many moral and ethical question.*
   (d) *Most young adult have problems of one kind or another.*
   (e) *Quite a few of these song promote violence.*

   Answers p. 248

C5 COUNTABLE AND UNCOUNTABLE NOUNS

1. **Many of the problems that Creole speakers have with number in English are to do with the different treatment of countable and uncountable nouns.**

   The class of words known as "nouns" can be divided into different subclasses. The most familiar subclasses are proper and common nouns. Proper nouns are the names of particular persons or things, written with a capital letter at the beginning: Sylvie, Aruna, Wednesday, France.

   There is another very important division that we must know about: some nouns refer to things that are **countable,** and some refer to things that cannot be counted.

   Nouns are therefore divided into two categories known as **countable** and **uncountable** nouns. (The latter are also called **mass** nouns.)

2. **Countable nouns** are names of things which can be counted, things which take the form of individual items:

   > marble, cat, child, university, member, relationship, solution

   Countable nouns are those which have a singular and a plural.

3. **Uncountable nouns** are names of things which cannot be counted, because they are seen as one mass or block, not separate items:

   > cloth, oil, dirt, soup, bread, information, dignity

   3.1 **Uncountable nouns can only be singular.**

   3.2 Most uncountable nouns are names of either materials, substances or abstract things.

   3.3 Some of the words that are seen as uncountable nouns in English really refer to countable items bunched together into one category. **Lumber, offspring** and **livestock,** for example, are all uncountable nouns. (More on this in C11.)

4. **There are some nouns which can be uncountable or countable:**

   A. (a) You spend too much **time** watching television.

   (b) This is the second **time** that this has happened.

   (c) They ran around the field three **times.**

   B. (a) The door is made of **glass.**

   (b) Give your grandmother a **glass** of water.

   (c) We have washed all the **glasses** and cups.

The nouns in bold type in the (a) sentences are uncountable nouns. Try making them plural in those sentences and you will find that they make no sense.

In (b) and (c) the same words become countable nouns, each with a singular and plural form – *and a different meaning.*

5. Uncountable nouns cannot be made plural; nor can they be used with the indefinite article a/an (see C6) which means "one". You cannot say "a furniture" or "an information". (More on this in C11).

You cannot properly acquire a language by learning off rules and ready-made lists of words. To sort out the sometimes tricky question of which nouns are seen as countable nouns, which are uncountable and which are both, you need to do plenty of reading and observe as you read. Make your own lists of countable, uncountable, and "two-way" nouns.

C5 Practice

1. Which of the following words are countable nouns, and which are uncountable nouns?

milk	rubbish	steel
streets	cigarettes	twelve months
oxygen	a highway	cocoa
a city	laziness	both villages
dirt	two pictures	labour
mosquitoes	clay	several students
smoke	justice	another cow
an earthquake	one chair	intelligence

2. Identify countable and uncountable nouns in *Disaster* (p. 3).

3. In the following sentences, there are five nouns, each of which appears three times. Each one appears in three different sentences: once as an uncountable noun, once as a singular countable noun and once as a plural countable noun.

   Identify these nouns and the three different ways in which each one is used. CLUE: one of them is **chicken.**

   (a) I prefer beef to chicken.
   (b) Experience has taught us many valuable lessons.
   (c) Many crimes are committed for the sake of money.
   (d) The guava tree is the place where the chickens have decided to sleep.
   (e) Those people have had an experience which they will not forget for the rest of their lives.

(f) You need a thicker oil for this purpose.

(g) It is true that beer has some food value.

(h) How do you intend to fry fish without oil?

(i) I don't think that one chicken is going to be enough.

(j) The book recounts the experiences of a young girl growing up in the early part of this century.

(k) Laziness is not yet counted as a crime.

(l) You can take another beer out of the fridge.

(m) They use various oils and perfumes in their ceremonies.

(n) Her friends dared her to go into the rumshop and order three beers.

(o) Crime does not pay.

Answers p. 249

C6 USE OF DETERMINERS

1. **Nouns are often introduced by the words referred to in A9, Noun slots 3.1.**

    These words are known as **determiners**.

    1.1 Uncountable nouns can be used without determiners:

    > This patient needs **oxygen**.
    > **Flour** is sold in shops and markets.
    > **Education** makes a big difference.

    1.2 Plural countable nouns can be used without determiners:

    > I have been collecting **spoons**.
    > He hates **dogs**.
    > **Elevators** can be dangerous.

    1.3 But **a singular countable noun *must* be introduced by a determiner.**

    In English you cannot say:

    > X Bring **spoon**.
    > X **Dog** is a good companion.
    > X **Elevator** is for lazy people.

Such a noun has to have in front of it an article **(the, a** or **an)** or one of the other determiners referred to in A9, **Noun slots** 3.1:

    X Bring **that spoon**.
    X **The dog** is a good companion.
    X **An elevator** is for lazy people.

2. **The most commonly-used determiners are the articles the, a, an.**

  2.1 **The** is called the **definite article.** It is used when both you and your listener know beforehand which item or items you are referring to:

    Bring **the spoon**.
    The doctors are holding a meeting.
    Put away **the butter** before it melts.

  2.2. The **indefinite article** is **a** (or **an** before vowels – see C7). It is used when the noun refers to one item but not a particular one – any one of that kind:

    Bring **a spoon**.
    A doctor has to sign this.
    The are going to install **an elevator**.

3. **CREOLE GRAMMAR**

> (a) The child don't even have **pencil**.
>
> (b) You think **vagrant** stupid!
>
> (c) Not everything you see in **book** you must believe.
>
> (d) Them fraid fe **duppy**.
>
> (e) You have **pickney**?
>
> The nouns in bold type are countable nouns.
>
> They have no plural markers (see C4), so we could say that they were singular countable nouns.
>
> But they have no determiners before them.
>
> In English only uncountable nouns, and plural nouns, can be used like this.
>
> What is special about these nouns is that they are neither singular nor plural, really.
>
> The speaker is not referring to one pencil, or vagrant, or to any particular number of them. It could be one, or it could be many.

> **Number does not matter in this situation.**
>
> With each of these nouns, the speaker is referring to a **class** of things or persons, not individual items.
>
> **Pencil** is treated as a "species": the noun has a **generic** meaning. So do all the other nouns in bold type above.
>
> In this situation, Creole treats countable nouns just like uncountable nouns: singular form and no article.
>
> In the opposite situation, i.e. to refer to specific items, Creole speakers do use the definite article:
>
>> You have the pencil I give you?
>>
>> They move all the vagrant and them from Frederick Street.

In Creole, then, a countable noun is used without a determiner and with nothing to show number when it doesn't matter which or how many items the noun refers to.

Note that this usage sometimes occurs in English:

>> **Man** is born free.
>> They have dropped out of **school**.

"Man" and "school" are countable nouns, used in their singular form, with no article. "Man" here does not refer to one male person; nor does "school" refer to just a building. Cases like these, however, are exceptions to the English rule.

4. **In the following sentences, students have carried the Creole rule over into English.** They have used singular countable nouns with no article, to refer to a whole class or kind of item:

    X (a) *Gas <u>mask</u> must be worn.*

    X (b) *This will create bad <u>relationship</u> among friends.*

    X (c) *It is a good thing to join <u>organization</u> for the betterment of the community.*

    X (d) *I prefer <u>apartment</u> to <u>house.</u>*

    X (e) *<u>Student</u> should not have to bear the full cost of university education.*

    4.1 In English, the usual way to show that you are referring to a class or kind of item rather than specific ones is to use the plural form of the noun without a determiner:

    (a) Gas **masks** must be worn.

    (b) This will create bad **relationships** among friends.

    (c) It is a good thing to join **organizations** for the betterment of the community.

(d) I prefer **apartments** to **houses**.

(e) **Students** should not have to bear the full cost of university education.

4.2 Another way is to use the singular form of the noun with the indefinite article, for this article shows that you are not referring to any one particular item of that kind:

(a) **A** gas **mask** must be worn.

(b) This will create **a** bad **relationship** among friends.

(c) It is a good thing to join **an organization** for the betterment of the community.

(d) I prefer **an apartment** to **a house**.

(e) **A student** should not have to bear the full cost of university education.

4.3 In some cases a singular countable noun can be used with the **definite** article to refer to the whole class or kind of item. (This is not the normal use of the definite article. See 2.1 above.)

The student should not have to bear the full cost of university education.

That television station has no respect for **the viewer**.

Do you know that **the cat** is a beast of prey?

The computer has revolutionized our world.

If the nouns in bold type are replaced by their plurals **without determiners** (as in 4.1 above) – **students, viewers, cats, computers** – the meaning remains the same.

5. **Proper nouns (names of particular people or things) are not normally used with determiners:**

Fitzroy has gone to **Barbados**.

C6 Practice

1. In the following sentences identify nouns with and without determiners (see A9, **Noun slots** 3.1). Say whether each noun is uncountable, singular countable or plural countable. For example:

    Students should not have to bear the full cost of university education.

Determiner	Noun	Description of Noun
	students	plural countable
the	cost	singular countable
	education	uncountable

    (**University** here is acting as an adjective. See D4.)

A. (a) Some dogs are afraid of thunder.
   (b) You look as if you've seen a ghost.
   (c) People have started to cultivate marijuana in that forest.
   (d) Yesterday we ate in a restaurant.
   (e) A bulldozer was mowing down the hill.

B. (a) An aeroplane flew over the islands.
   (b) This month eggs are scarce.
   (c) You can find that information in a book.
   (d) Books provide knowledge and enjoyment.
   (e) This is the first time that they have been late.

C. (a) Take your raincoat with you.
   (b) He was seeing dots before his eyes.
   (c) That firm assembles cars.
   (d) The love of money is the root of all evil.
   (e) They want to hold an early election.

2. Identify and correct the number errors in the following sentences, either by putting in an article (**the, a, an**) where necessary, or by making the noun plural:

A. (a) *This leaves lasting effect on the personality.*

(b) *In the 1970s trade union had a lot of bargaining power.*

(c) *There is no clear-cut definition for such term.*

(d) *Another cause of road accident is negligence.*

(e) *Only a few will obtain job when they leave school.*

B. (a) *The government of our country and certain organization in the society should work together to solve this problem.*

(b) *Survival is the ability to live through new and usually difficult situation via adaptation.*

(c) *You can see flowers blooming at the different housing development.*

(d) *It is this way of life for women that has brought about women's movement in some countries.*

(e) *Such institution would cater more efficiently to the needs of the people.*

C. (a) *Infant mortality rate will be greatly reduced.*

(b) *This can cause a decrease in number of accidents.*

(c) *Drugs can break down family unit.*

(d) *With the introduction of cess, university education became even more expensive.*

(e) *Such student are offered scholarship to the local University of the West Indies and some are also offered scholarship to universities abroad.*

Answers pp. 249-250

C7 ARTICLES: WHEN TO USE *AN*

1. **The *an* form of the indefinite article (see C6:2.2) is not used in Creole and so needs our special attention.**

   A and **an** mean the same thing.

   1.1 **A** is the form used before words beginning with a consonant (any letter except a, e, i, o, or u).

   1.2 **An** is the form used before words beginning with a vowel - a, e, i, o, or u - or a silent **h**: an achievement, an egg, an interest, an oven, an uncle, an honour.

2. **The letter u at the beginning of a word is not always sounded as a vowel.** It has two different pronunciations:
   (a) uncle, umbrella, ulcer
   (b) university, uniform, union

   In (a) the **u** is a true vowel.

In (b) the **u** is pronounced like the word **you**, which means that these words begin with the consonant sound **y**.

Where the **u** at the beginning of a word has this "**you**" sound, the article **a** is used.

a university, a uniform, a union.

3. **Sometimes other words may come between the article and the noun which it introduces.**
Then the word immediately following the article is the one that tells us whether to use **a** or **an**, not the noun itself:

He put an egg in his lunchkit.
He put a boiled egg in his lunchkit.

They have made a proposal.
They have made an utterly ridiculous proposal.

4. **In Creole there is only one form of the indefinite article.**
A is used before all words, whatever sound they begin with: "a orange, a bun, a egg".

5. **Jamaican speakers often add an "h" sound before words beginning with a vowel, and drop "h" when it begins a word: "enter" becomes "henter", and "higgler" becomes "iggler". When using English beware of this, or you could make mistakes with a and an:**

X *An* higgler is *a* entrepreneur.

C7 Practice

Put the article **a** or **an** before each of the following phrases:

A. (a) unofficial report
   (b) unique form of protest
   (c) excellent piece of work
   (d) heir to the throne
   (e) young offender

B. (a) guardian angel
   (b) hour later
   (c) effort to discredit the politician
   (d) unified force
   (e) meeting of athletes

C. (a) foreign university
   (b) interim committee
   (c) honest day's work
   (d) health centre
   (e) arriving passenger

Answers p. 250

C8 NOUNS WITH QUANTITY EXPRESSIONS

1. **Nouns are often used with other words which tell us how much or how many.** These words are usually placed before the noun. We shall call these **quantity expressions**.

    1.1 Some quantity expressions mean "one" (e.g. **one, each, every, another**). Naturally, these are followed by singular nouns only.

    1.2 Some (such as **several, many, both** and numbers from **two** upwards) are followed by plural nouns only.

    1.3 Others, however, are sometimes followed by singular nouns and sometimes by plural nouns, and this creates a certain amount of confusion for Creole speakers using English. In Creole, as we have seen (C4), nouns have the same form whether they refer to one item or more.

2. **The answer to this problem is really quite simple, and is again to do with the difference between countable and uncountable nouns:**

    (a) Put **some water** on the table.
    (b) Put **some plates** on the table.

    (a) You haven't taken **enough time** over this.
    (b) There aren't **enough seats** in the room.

    (a) **All rubbish** must be put into bins.
    (b) **All students** must report to their classrooms.

The quantity expressions **some**, **enough**, and **all** are followed by singular nouns in the (a) sentences, and plural nouns in the (b) sentences.

In (a) the nouns in bold type are uncountable. An uncountable noun is always singular, whatever quantity expression is used with it. In (b) the nouns in bold type are countable. A countable noun used with a quantity expression has to be plural, usually. If, however, the quantity expression means "one", then the noun is singular:

each table, every seat, another student.

3. **There are many quantity expressions which end with the word of, and some of them are used in the same way as those above:**

   (a) Some of the food
   (b) Some of the tomatoes

   (a) A lot of courage
   (b) A lot of ashtrays

   (a) Most of the lumber
   (b) Most of the problems

   > **NB:** Even those that are made up of words meaning "one", plus **of**, are *always* followed by plural countable nouns:
   >
   > Each child... BUT: Each of the children... (see C9).

4. **Some quantity expressions can be used in three ways:** with uncountable nouns, as in the (a) sentences above; with plural countable nouns as in the (b) sentences above, *and* with singular countable nouns as in the following sentences:

   > **Most of the day** was spent in silence.
   > Termites have taken over **all of the floor**.
   > I've seen **enough of this film**.

   What is important is the meaning of what you are saying. The phrase in bold type in each sentence here focuses on the whole or part of **one** thing. The noun that names that thing must therefore be singular.

   Compare each of the following sentences with its counterpart above:

   > **Most of the days** were spent in silence.
   > Termites have taken over **all of the floors**.
   > I've seen **enough of these films**.

5.   **CREOLE GRAMMAR**

In Creole we use the quantity expressions **much** and **amount of** with all nouns, countable or uncountable.

> How much **gas** you want?
>
> How much **cigarette** you want?
>
> Well, the amount of **mud** come down...
>
> When we see the amount of **mango**...

6. In English **much** and **amount of** cannot be used with countable nouns.

   6.1 **Much** and **amount of** should only be used with uncountable nouns:

   (a) I have put too **much salt** in the soup.

   (b) The investigation revealed a certain **amount of corruption**.

   6.2 **Many, many of** and **number of** are used to introduce plural countable nouns:

   (a) I have put too **many ornaments** on that shelf.

   (b) The investigation revealed a certain **number of irregularities**.

7. Like some other quantity expressions with of (see 4. above), much of can be used with singular countable nouns where the meaning requires it.

   Much of the day was spent in silence.

8. **The majority of can only be used with plural countable nouns:**

   The majority of cases come from this area.

Once more, plenty of reading and observation will help you sort out how to use quantity expressions in English.

C8 Practice

1. Use each of the words given under the sentence to fill in the blank space. Say the sentences aloud before you write them down:

A. (a) Some of the _____ was destroyed in the fire.
   furniture, information, luggage, machinery, lumber

   (b) Some of the _____ were destroyed in the fire.
   chairs, records, suitcases, machines, boards

B. (a) They put all the _____ into a bag.
   money, jewelry, flour, rice, equipment

   (b) They put all the _____ into a bag.
   keys, bottles, things, shoes, plants

2. Use each quantity expression on the left with each of the nouns on the right, **making the noun plural when necessary.**

For example:

    (a) a lot of fun, a lot of pencils

Say them aloud before you write them down.

(a) a lot of	fun, pencil, question, work, concrete
(b) some	shoe, cocoa, meat, problem, appointment
(c) enough	hand, asphalt, town, teacher, name, rum, letter, smoke, button, leather

3. Now introduce each of the nouns in the box above with either **too much** or **too many**.

   Make sure that you choose the right one for each noun, and that you make the noun plural when necessary.

   For example:

       too much fun, too many pencils

4. Use each of the phrases given under the sentence to fill in the blank space. Say the sentences aloud before you write them down:

   A. We need to reduce the amount of _____ there is in this country.
   domestic violence, alcohol abuse, illegal squatting, religious intolerance, juvenile delinquency, drug trafficking, racial prejudice, organized crime, sexual harassment, praedial larceny

   B. We need to reduce the number of _____ there are in this country.
   road accidents, public holidays, violent crimes, high school dropouts, homeless people, roadside vendors, unlicensed firearms, squatters' settlements, stray dogs, unemployed people

5. In each of the following sentences the wrong quantity expression is used. Correct these errors, saying the corrected sentences aloud before writing them down.

   (a) *An alarming amount of young people are abusing drugs.*

   (b) *Many of our vegetation will have to be cleared to support an increased human population.*

   (c) *She has always tried to help as much people as possible.*

   (d) *The present building can only accommodate a limited amount of vendors.*

   (e) *Many of the equipment will be obsolete in a few years' time.*

6. In these sentences **the majority of** is wrongly used. In some sentences this quantity expression can be replaced by **most,** and in others by **most of**.

Choose the appropriate expression, saying the corrected sentences aloud before writing them down.

(a) *The majority of Caribbean music shows African influence.*

(b) *This programme is for people who spend the majority of their day indoors.*

(c) *Here it is warm and dry for the majority of the year.*

(d) *The majority of praedial larceny takes place during these hours.*

(e) *For the majority of the time he sat staring into space.*

Answers p. 251

C9 ONE OF...

The following is a very common error in the writing of Caribbean users of English:

X *One of the <u>neighbour</u> went on holiday.*

One of is **NOT** the same as **one**. When you say "one neighbour", you are referring to a single neighbour. When you use **one of**, however, you are singling out that neighbour from among a number of neighbours. You cannot sensibly speak of one among one.

Words which mean "one" must be followed by plural nouns when they are used with **of**:

Each child   BUT: Each of the children
Another problem   BUT: Another of our problems
One house   BUT: One of these houses
One neighbour went on holiday   BUT: One of the **neighbours** went on holiday.

One of, each of and **another of** must always be followed by the plural.

C9 Practice

Use each of the words given under the sentence to fill in the blank space. Say the sentences aloud before you write them down:

1. A. One of the _____ chaired the meeting.
    doctors, women, lawyers, calypsonians, children, drivers, students, sisters, ministers, nurses

    B. They have misplaced one of the _____ .
    buckets, cards, files, parts, programmes, chairs, needles, tickets, screwdrivers, lamps

    C. That is one of their most important _____ .
    challenges, concerns, successes, accomplishments, milestones, considerations, stages, discoveries, principles, ingredients

2. Each of the _____ was examined carefully.
    patients, options, theories, immigrants, proposals, products, containers, exhibits, labels, items

3. This article highlights another of the _____ emerging in the country.
    developments, conflicts, movements, groupings, trends, phenomena, campaigns, problems, controversies, fads

4. Correct the noun introduced by **one of** in each of the following sentences:

    (a) *Inefficiency is one of the main reason why many countries are facing financial difficulties.*

    (b) *Cocaine is one of the most destructive "hard drug".*

    (c) *The German shepherd is one of the largest dog in the canine family.*

    (d) *The 19th of November 1989 can he considered one of the greatest day in the history of sport for Trinidad and Tobago.*

    (e) *This is only one of the major disadvantage you will face.*

Answers p. 251

C10 NOUNS ENDING WITH A SOUND LIKE S

1. **Caribbean users of English sometimes leave off the plural ending when a noun already ends with a sound like s.** There is the feeling that the word is already plural because it ends with this sound.

    Here are some examples of this error:

    X (a) *I want to take some <u>course</u> at UWI.*

    X (b) *All the <u>airhostess</u> came off the plane.*

    X *(c) We had to make ten <u>sentence</u> for homework.*

    X *(d) Hundreds of <u>tourist</u> landed today.*

    In the case of sentence (d), the noun in fact ends with a **t**. But English words which end with **st** end with an **s** sound in Creole. The English words **tourist, artist** and **vest** in Creole are:

    "touriss", "artiss" and "vess".

    In each of the underlined words in the sentences above, (a) to (d), the **s** sound at the end is **part of the word itself,** so we still have to add an **s** to make the plural.

2. **When you put the s onto words which end in s, se, or ce, they gain an extra syllable for easier pronunciation (see C2:2):**

    hostess-es, cours-es, sentenc-es.

3. **But words ending in st do not gain an extra syllable and these plurals are, for us, a little difficult to pronounce:**

    tourists, artists, vests.

    (Some Creole speakers solve the problem by saying "tourisses", "artisses" and "vesses", but these are wrong!)

    The English pronunciation of such plurals **(tourists, artists, vests)** needs practice. At any rate, even if you find these plurals hard to pronounce, make sure that you **write** them correctly. **Do not leave off the s.**

C10 Practice

1. Make the following nouns plural.

   Say the plurals aloud and then write them down.

test	disguise	phrase	convenience
place	wrist	guest	vest
quiz	address	trace	class
circumstance	post	prize	artist
list	disc	breast	ghost
exercise	pianist	appliance	nurse
glass	loss	task	face

2. In each of these sentences there is a plural noun without its plural ending. Correct these errors.

   (a) *The owners of these business are not taxed.*

   (b) *These are the consequence of drunk driving.*

   (c) *It has been many long years that scientist and researchers have been working on a cure for AIDS.*

   (d) *Place like villages situated deep in the country may not have a reliable supply of electricity.*

   (e) *The pupils' desk were arranged in neat rows.*

   Answers p. 251

C11 SOME PROBLEM NOUNS

1. Uncountable nouns for countable things

   1.1 Uncountable nouns, as we have seen, are always singular (see C5). Therefore we must never add an **s** to a noun unless it is a countable noun.

   Here are some uncountable nouns to which some people mistakenly add an **s**:

equipment	offspring	garbage
aircraft	baggage	prey
furniture	luggage	scenery
gravel	apparel	foodstuff
print	personnel	livestock

   In English these nouns must never be given an **s** ending.

The problem is that these nouns are often mistaken for countable nouns, for each of them refers to a collection of individual items. For example, **furniture** means chairs, tables, desks, beds, etc., which are separate items and can be easily counted.

In English, however, these words are treated as uncountable nouns, and are never turned into the plural.

1.2 This poses a second problem. How do you refer to one item in the collection? You cannot say:

> X *an equipment; a furniture; a scenery.*

With some of these nouns you can refer to one item by using "a piece of":

> a piece of equipment/furniture/gravel/baggage/luggage/apparel

With others you can't, and you solve the problem by using another word entirely:

offspring	–	a child
personnel	–	an employee/worker/member of staff
scenery	–	a scene

2. Plural form only

2.1 On the other hand there are some nouns which in English are always in the plural form, but are not all plural:

A	B
news	scissors
politics	pants
mathematics	glasses
economics	spectacles

Nouns in Column A are uncountable nouns, therefore singular. Those in B are plural countable nouns, which means that you can have one or many of the things referred to.

2.2 Again, therefore, there is the problem of how to make them singular. You can't take off the **s** ending!

Americans take the **s** off **pants** to make it singular, but this is not accepted as Standard English in the Caribbean.

"A spectacle" and "a glass" have nothing to do with the thing you wear on your face to see better.

And there is no such thing as "a scissor".

You refer to *one* of these things by using "a pair of..." – a pair of scissors/pants/spectacles/glasses.

3. CREOLE GRAMMAR

3.1 Some nouns which are always plural in English are treated as both singular and plural in Creole. So when we need to use them in the singular, we use them as they are, **s** ending and all:

a scissors, a pants, a glasses, a jeans, a sliders

(You can't do this in Standard English!)

3.2 This is also done in Creole with the following nouns which *do* have a singular form in English:

a flowers, a ants, a peas, a shoes, a slippers, a sneakers, a lice, a mice, a teeth.

CII Practice

Correct the number errors in these sentences:

A. (a) *Customs officers check certain baggages very carefully.*

(b) *The cricket bat is a very unique sporting equipment.*

(c) *The business people in this city throw all their garbages onto the pavements.*

(d) *He is painting a tropical scenery.*

(e) *It is time to rearrange the furnitures.*

B. (a) *The youngster was wearing a very expensive sneakers.*

(b) *In the sewing class one scissors is shared by five pupils.*

(c) *Lystra Williams was last seen wearing a blue pants and a white top.*

(d) *The cleaner found a glasses on the floor.*

(e) *Since we got these cats we haven't seen one single mice in the house.*

Answers pp. 251-252

D. Possession

D1 FORMING THE POSSESSIVE

1. **The possessive form of a noun (or pronoun) is that form which shows possession or ownership.** (More on pronouns in Level 2 of this manual.)

    You use the possessive form to show that persons or things own other persons or things:

    (a) **Marjorie's** books

    (b) the **lion's** den

    (c) the **nurses'** quarters

    (d) two **brothers'** children

    In (a) and (b) the possessive nouns (in bold type) are singular in number.

    In (c) and (d) they are plural.

2. **The possessive marker in English is an s sound added at the end of a noun.** In writing the possessive form of a noun you put an s ending and a punctuation mark – an apostrophe.

3. **Singular**

    When the name of the owner is singular, the **s** ending is separated from the word by the apostrophe:

    Trevor's case   **the dog's** tail
    St Lucia's national debt **a person's** rights

    (An apostrophe has the same shape as a comma, but hangs just above the level of the common letters. It goes into the space *after* a letter – it does not sit on top of one letter.)

4. **Plural**

    When the name of the owner is a regular plural noun (i.e., with an **s** ending) you simply place an apostrophe after the **s**:

    nurses' quarters   the **Parmasads'** daughter
    boys' shoes   the **unions'** position

5. **Irregular plurals**

    What about nouns which make their plural differently, i.e. those which do not take an **s** ending, such as **children** or **media**?

To make the possessive of these nouns you do the same as for singular nouns. You add an **s** ending, separated from the word by an apostrophe:

children's toys   the **women's** movement
those **people's** gardens.

6. Nouns ending in s

How do you make the possessive when the noun already ends with an **s**, for example **Thomas, stewardess, boss**?

6.1 For the spoken form of the possessive you add an **es** sound – an extra syllable. The three words given here are pronounced in the possessive, "Thomas-es", "stewardess-es", and "boss-es".

6.2 Two written forms exist:

- **Either** add an apostrophe and nothing else, as you do with plural nouns (regular): **Thomas'** house; the **stewardess'** name; the **boss'** orders.

- **Or** add an apostrophe and then an **s**, as you do with any other singular noun:

Thomas's house; the **stewardess's** name; the **boss's** orders

The first form (apostrophe only) is less acceptable today.

7. NB: In English you cannot say:

X *these children's stomach*

X *the workers' salary*

X *the nurses' husband*

7.1 The underlined nouns cannot be singular because each child has a stomach, each worker a salary, and so on. More than one owner means more than one of the items owned:

these children's stomachs

the workers' salaries

the nurses' husbands

7.2 It is quite in order, however, to speak of

these children's mother

the workers' goal

the nurses' lunchroom

for one mother, one goal and one lunchroom can be shared among a number of owners.

7.3 And, of course, if the noun that names the owned item is an uncountable noun, then it is singular, even if the owner is plural, because uncountable nouns are always singular:

> the nurses' dignity

8. Note how the possessive is used to refer to a period of time:

> a month's notice
>
> in five days' time
>
> three weeks' leave

D1 Practice

1. Identify possessive nouns in the following sentences. Say whether each possessive noun is singular or plural.
   (a) The judge rejected the lawyer's submission and dismissed her client's case.
   (b) Mr Oliver was a founding member of the postmen's union formed fifty years ago.
   (c) Under this system, high school graduates are given two years' training as teachers' aides.
   (d) The political leader made an appeal to the party's rank-and-file members.
   (e) Funds are being raised to send the school's football team to Jamaica.

2. Turn the nouns on the left into the possessive form and use them to introduce each of the nouns on the right, in turn.

   For example: a baby's clothes, a baby's skills, a baby's mother. Say the phrases aloud and then write them down.

A. (a) a baby	clothes, skills, mother, weight, development, food, chair, face, health, demands
(b) Asha	
(c) the artist	
(d) Garvin	
(e) Mr Inniss	

B. (a) most people	habits, time, homes,
(b) Rastafarians	labour, opinions, faces,
(c) some teachers	behaviour, responsibilities,
(d) the men	intelligence, jobs
(e) these ladies	

3. Fill the blank slot in each sentence with the possessive forms of the nouns given, one at a time.

   Say each sentence aloud before you write it down.

   (a) A kitchen garden can help to lower a _____ food bills. (family, person, household)

   (b) The _____ picture appeared on the television screen. (actress, fugitive, suspect)

   (c) Some _____ car tyres were slashed. (members, customers, lecturers)

   (d) I think that _____ reaction is likely to be positive. (the board, Chris, my colleague)

   (e) The research team is gathering information on _____ pastimes. (children, pensioners, consumers)

   Answers pp. 252-253

D2 FORMING THE POSSESSIVE WITH *OF*

1. There is another way of forming the possessive.

Instead of adding an **s** to the name of the owner, we can use the preposition **of** to show the possessive relationship between two nouns:

>   the neighbours' noise OR
>   the noise of the neighbours

>   women's equality OR
>   the equality of women

>   the girl's friends OR
>   the friends of the girl.

2. It is more convenient to use this form when the name of the owner is a longish phrase.
Instead of

> Marcus Garvey Memorial College's principal

(which would be very clumsy), you say:

> the principal of Marcus Garvey Memorial College.

3. When the name of the owner is modified by a clause (See B6) we have to use the of form:

> the name of the student who failed the exam

> NOT: X *the student who failed the exam's name*

> NOR: X *the student's name who failed the exam*

4. This method of forming the possessive is also more suitable than the s ending when the owner is abstract:

These are all rather clumsy phrases:

> experience's voice
> education's goals
> colonialism's legacy

They can all be improved by using **of**:

> the voice of experience
> the goals of education
> the legacy of colonialism

5. It is often more appropriate to use of when the owner is an inanimate object – a thing which is not alive:

> the thickness of paper
> the colour of the table
> the face of a clock

D2 Practice

Correct or improve these sentences by using the possessive formed with **of**:

A. (a) *This film shows how the man who got hit body reacted to the blow.*
   (b) *We have the capacity to exploit this universe's resources.*
   (c) *The band's sponsor's name was announced on the opening night.*
   (d) *Television networks income comes mainly from advertising.*
   (e) *This can cause further parent-child relations breakdown.*

B. (a) *Nobody could remember the person's name heading the committee.*
   (b) *We do not give sufficient thought to terminally ill patients presence in our society.*
   (c) *Public schools classrooms are overcrowded.*
   (d) *Fibre optics major application is in the field of telecommunications.*
   (e) *We ought not to expect any dramatic improvement in the tourist industry's growth.*

C. (a) *The visiting lecturer spoke on the African National Congress role in dismantling apartheid.*
   (b) *These activities significantly contribute to the Natural Science student all-round education.*
   (c) *Trinidad and Tobago's population's cosmopolitan character is the subject of much discussion.*
   (d) *The research paper's organization is not very good.*
   (e) *Listeners calling in to the programme are asked to lower their radios' volume or to turn them off entirely.*

Answers p. 253

D3 THE POSSESSIVE: COMMON ERRORS

1. Before we look at the errors we make with possessive nouns in Standard English, we should look at how the possessive is expressed in Creole.

   ### CREOLE GRAMMAR

   > (a) That is **Mildred** house.
   > (b) Is who move the **teacher** chair?
   > (c) The **nurse** and them lunchroom upstairs.
   >
   > Each of the words in bold type names an owner. Each of these is therefore a possessive noun. There is nothing in the word itself to show that it is possessive. So how can we tell, in Creole, when a noun is possessive?
   >
   > (i) *Word order.* The owner is placed right before what is owned: **Mildred** is placed before **house**.
   >
   > (ii) *Intonation.* This word means the "tune" of speech. Say aloud the pairs of nouns in bold print:
   >
   >   (a) the **boy-friend** (meaning "lover")
   >   (b) the **boy friend** (the friend of the boy)
   >
   >   (a) **Mammy-apple** (the fruit)
   >   (b) **Mammy apple** (the apple which belongs to Mammy)
   >
   >   (a) a **horse-face** man (a man with a face like that of a horse)
   >   (b) the **horse face** (the face of the horse)
   >
   >   In (b) the first noun is possessive. Do you detect the special intonation?
   >
   > (iii) *Stress.* Notice, too, the differences in stress, i.e. which parts are emphasized.

2. What are the errors that Caribbean people make with possessive nouns in English?

   ### 2.1 *Missing ending*

   First and foremost, Caribbean people tend to carry over the Creole rule into English, placing nouns side by side to show possession. We forget that in English the possessive noun has a special marker:

   X (a) This <u>student</u> work is of a very high standard.

2.2 Missing apostrophe

Or, in writing, we may remember the **s** but forget the apostrophe:

X (b) *Who is the Caribbeans greatest cricketer?*

2.3 Misplaced apostrophe

Sometimes we put the apostrophe in the wrong place:

X (c) *These farmer's crops have been destroyed by floods.*

2.4 Misplaced ending

Sometimes the possessive ending is put on the wrong noun:

X (d) *The builder tool's were stolen.*

2.5 Plural for possessive

Because the possessive ending is an **s** sound, some people think that the possessive is the same as the plural. This produces different errors:

2.5.1 People sometimes make a singular noun plural in order to make it possessive:

X (e) *A person is influenced by societies values.*

2.5.2 When the noun is already plural, the **s** ending of the written form is seen as enough to make it possessive. No apostrophe is used:

X (f) *People living in apartments have to put up with all their neighbours noise.*

2.5.3 Even irregular plurals (without **s**) are often used just as they are for the possessive:

X (g) *The visitor gave a talk on women equality with men.*

2.6 Apostrophe for no reason

2.6.1 People sometimes decorate a plural noun with an apostrophe, making the noun possessive when it is not:

X (h) *Stove's repaired here*

2.6.2 Some people even make the mistake of putting an apostrophe on a verb with an **s** ending:

X (i) *Cocaine destroy's the brain.*

D3 Practice

1. Correct the errors identified in sentences (a) to (i) above.

2. Correct the errors made with the possessive in the following sentences:

A. (a) *Who is sitting at the receptionist desk?*
   (b) *These television programmes are putting all kinds of ideas into young viewer's heads.*
   (c) *Smoking has disastrous effects on the human being lungs, heart and entire respiratory system.*
   (d) *Young people today face greater challenge's than their parents did in their youth.*
   (e) *The puppies mother takes very good care of them.*

B. (a) *The nation productivity is at a low level.*
   (b) *Dogs coats vary in colour.*
   (c) *The sun ray's travel through outer space.*
   (d) *We have some new children books on display.*
   (e) *There would not be so many accidents on the road if motorist's took more care.*

C. (a) *The child academic grade's began to fall.*
   (b) *People standard of living has been lowered.*
   (c) *She work's very hard at her job.*
   (d) *Such a move will only endanger the two hostage's lives.*
   (e) *We got a birds eye view of the village.*

Answers p. 253

D4 POSSESSIVE NOUNS V. ADJECTIVAL NOUNS

1. **When they are writing English, Caribbean people sometimes place nouns side by side without using the s ending to show possession, because that is how it is done in Creole (see D3).**

   But in English you do often see nouns placed one after the other with no possessive ending on the first noun:

   (a) a department store
   (b) football jerseys
   (c) the student body
   (d) a Kitchener calypso

   These phrases are all correct English usage.

   In phrases such as these, the first noun is **not** a possessive noun. If you try to make the first noun possessive, what you will get is some nonsense phrases, or, you will get a totally different meaning: "the student body" is not the same as "the student's body".

   "The student body" means the whole collection of students attending a particular school.

   "The student's body" means the body (dead or alive) of a student.

   In the phrases (a) to (d) above, the first noun is acting as an adjective. It indicates not an owner, but a **type**. In (a), **department** tells us that the store is not a **book** store, or a **drug** store, but the type of store that is divided into departments.

   Often the adjectival noun and the noun which it modifies are joined together to make one noun:

   > canefield, bathroom, rainbow, sunlight, suitcase

2. **WARNING! Note that in English a noun acting as an adjective is usually in the singular.**
   Do not make it plural. You would never think of saying, for example, "feetball" or "teethbrush".

   Yet we cannot say that adjectival nouns are never plural, for in some cases they are: **skills training; the Airports Authority; the Examinations Section**. Again, reading and observation will help you familiarize yourself with the exceptions.

3. CREOLE GRAMMAR

> Some nouns have been adopted into Creole from English in their plural form. They are always used in that form, whether their meaning is singular or plural. (See C11:3.) Some of these nouns are used as adjectives, just as they are:
>
> the currants roll
> a flowers garden
> the shoes cupboard
> a ants nest
> some peas soup
> four nuts cake
>
> **These phrases cannot be carried over into English.**

In English the Creole phrases given above are:

the currant roll
a flower garden
the shoe cupboard
an ant nest
some pea soup
four nut cakes

D4 Practice

1. Identify adjectival nouns in these sentences:

A. (a) We are raising funds to donate to the Salvation Army.

(b) My aunt gave me a cricket bat for Christmas.

(c) They have to get a new telephone directory, for the one they have is out of date.

(d) We were insured, but the insurance company refused to pay.

(e) The Trinidad Carnival is a great tourist attraction.

B. (a) I can't imagine why dog collars should cost so much money.

(b) Medical science has made great strides in the area of organ transplants.

(c) People now know better than to take election promises seriously.

(d) The Agriculture students go on regular field trips as part of their training.

(e) There were bullet wounds all over the bandit's body.

C. (a) They couldn't find the way to the union hall.

   (b) Then at the traffic light they would have to turn left.

   (c) The Mighty Calamity has won the calypso competition again this year.

   (d) They made themselves some cheese sandwiches.

   (e) That television station has no respect for the viewer.

2. Correct errors made with adjectival nouns in the following sentences:

   (a) *The authorities have persuaded the apples vendors to shift their stalls to a new location.*

   (b) *Samuel Selvon is a short stories writer as well as a novelist.*

   (c) *We will be putting in louvres windows when we renovate the house.*

   (d) *Police blame these accidents on poor roads conditions.*

   (e) *They are part of the drugs prevention campaign in their community.*

Answers p. 254

Verb Forms

E. The Present Simple Tense

E1 FORMING THE PRESENT SIMPLE TENSE

1. Review A4:7. Tense.

> Ma Charlotte always **walks** to the market.
> Some teachers **walk** to school every day.

The words in bold type in these two sentences are verbs in the present simple tense.

2. How do we form this tense?

The form of the present simple tense is the same as the form of the infinitive (see A4:3) without **to**. Sometimes an **s** ending must be added.

The present simple tense, therefore, has two forms – the unmarked form and the form with an **s** added. Here are some examples:

Infinitive	Present simple tense	
to wait	1. wait	2. waits
to say	1. say	2. says
to hesitate	1. hesitate	2. hesitates

For the verb **to have** the two forms are: 1. have 2. has.

The verb **to be** is a law unto itself and is dealt with separately. (See E5.)

3. When to use form No. 1 of the present simple tense and when to use form No. 2 is a major problem for Caribbean users of English, who are not always sure when to add the s. This is the main problem that will be tackled in Section E.

E1 Practice

1. Give the two present simple tense forms of the verbs listed below.

    (i) Convert the verb into the infinitive.

    (ii) Remove the **to**. That gives you form No. 1 of the present simple tense.

    (iii) Add **s** for form No. 2 of the present simple tense.

For example – *succeeded:*

(i) to succeed (ii) succeed (iii) succeeds

(Remember that when the verb consists of more than one word, the last word is the main verb. See **A4:6**, and **A4 Practice** 1.)

A. (a) succeeded
    (b) happening
    (c) stolen
    (d) described
    (e) taught

B. (a) will increase
    (b) have taken
    (c) are fighting
    (d) flown
    (e) stained

C. (a) written
    (b) were constructing
    (c) belonged
    (d) sat
    (e) spun

2. Identify present simple tense verbs in the following sentences:

A. (a) Our panside celebrates its tenth anniversary next week.

   (b) All of our members live in LaGrange or in communities nearby.

   (c) Mr Barnes controls everything.

   (d) That television station has no respect for the viewer.

   (e) Government Ministries owe large sums of money to the Water and Sewerage Authority.

B. (a) Sylvester operates a bar on weekends.

   (b) They rarely misbehave in her house.

   (c) Today the school looks practically new.

   (d) At night the animals sleep under the house.

   (e) Ms Ramdeen chairs the general meeting.

C. (a) Ma remains the boss.

   (b) His latest calypso sounds really good.

   (c) They use various oils and perfumes in their ceremonies.

   (d) Whenever that dog hears a vehicle approaching, it rushes out into the road.

   (e) Children prefer these.

Answers p. 254

E2 USES OF THE PRESENT SIMPLE TENSE

1. This form has many uses or functions.

   1.1 Its main function is to show that an action takes place **all the time** or **regularly.** This is known as **habitual action**:

   (a) The earth **spins** on its axis.

   (b) Nurses **work** very hard.

   (c) Babies **cry** when they are hungry.

   (d) She **works** in the garden on weekends.

   1.2 Sometimes the present simple form of the verb is used to tell of something which will take place **in the future**:

   (e) Exams **begin** in two weeks' time.

   (f) We are practising a song for when the Minister of Education **visits** our school.

   (g) When you **write** your mother, give her my regards.

   (h) Wait here until they **come** back.

   1.3 Sometimes the present simple tense is used to dramatize an event that took place **in the past**:

   (i) This car **comes** speeding down the highway, **picks** up a skid, and BAM! It **spins** out of control.

   (j) Faced with mounting opposition, the President finally **resigns**.

2. You can see that it is not really true to say that the present simple tense is for actions taking place now, in the present. So far we have seen that this tense can be used for habitual action, future action and past action.

The present simple is not the most appropriate tense for action taking place in the present moment. For this we are more likely to use the other present tense form: the present continuous tense (see H2). If you are sitting with a plate of food in front of you and somebody phones to ask what you are doing, you are not likely to answer: "I eat my lunch". You are more likely to say: "I'm eating my lunch".

3. However, there are some situations in which the present simple tense is used to show present action:

> 3.1 It is the tense you would use with verbs which tell of **mental action** in the present, verbs such as: to know, to want, to prefer, to feel, to agree, to like, to love, to believe, to wish.
>
> (k) I **agree** with that suggestion.
>
> (l) These little children **know** the answer.
>
> (m) He **feels** a little foolish.
>
> (n) She **wants** one of those.
>
> 3.2 The present simple tense is used in the **live reporting** of events, for example ball-by-ball or blow-by-blow sports commentaries on radio or television:
>
> (o) Peterson **bowls** to Maraj.
>
> (p) Now the cortège **approaches** the cemetery.

E2 Practice

Identify the present simple tense verbs in the following sentences: What is the function of the present simple tense in each batch A – E?

A. (a) Those people really live a hard life.
 (b) You never finish your homework.
 (c) The telephone rings incessantly.
 (d) Michael and his sister sing in the church choir.
 (e) It only takes a minute.

B. (a) We should not give up until we find a solution.
 (b) The funeral takes place tomorrow.
 (c) You will be allowed those privileges when you learn to be responsible.
 (d) They are trying to finish the house before the rainy season starts.
 (e) The cricketers leave for the airport in the next half hour.

Present Simple Tense **E3**

C. (a) In October of 1983, the USA invades Grenada.

(b) At the sound of the police siren, instead of stopping, he puts on more speed.

(c) Eventually they find their way out of the bush and flag down a passing vehicle.

(d) Then she turns to the principal and gives him a piece of her mind.

(e) Within a matter of months the opposition parties join together, the government falls, and new policies come into effect.

D. (a) My sister and I like this house.

(b) She knows where to find the key.

(c) The manager wishes to speak with you.

(d) We prefer to wait here.

(e) The neighbours want to make an overseas call.

E. (a) Ingleton takes the catch at mid-on.

(b) Her Excellency Mrs Hassanali steps forward and lays her wreath at the cenotaph.

(c) Egyptian Princess moves into the lead but Shooting Star sticks close behind her.

(d) Scherzando, the reigning champions, carefully roll their pans on stage.

(e) The Regiment Band strikes up the National Anthem.

Answers p. 255

E3 WHEN TO PUT THE *S*

1. Go back to E2:1 and E2:3.

Identify the subject of each verb in bold type in the sentences (a) to (p), pp. 93-94

Draw up two columns. In these two columns list the subjects according to which form of the verb is used with each:

1 Subjects used with bare verb	2 Subjects used with verb + **s** ending

Before you go further, check whether your table is correct: answer on p. 255.

2. **Study this table and see whether you can find out from it when and when not to add s to verbs in the present simple tense.**

   Do not read further until you think you have found an answer.

3. **In column 1 you have both plural and singular subjects. In column 2 all the subjects are singular.**

   Is it then safe to say that you have to put an **s** on the verb when the subject is singular? But then what about the singular subjects in column 1?

   What are the singular subjects in column 1? There are only two: **you** and **I**. Everything else in column 1 is plural. **You** and **I** are exceptions in column 1, and **you** is used for both singular and plural. (See F8:2.)

4. **Now we can form the rule, known as subject-verb agreement:**

   Add an **s** to the verb in the present simple tense when its subject is singular, except for the subjects **you** and **I**.

5. **There is another way of expressing this rule.**

   All the subjects in column 2 have two things in common: **number** and **person**.

   Their number, as we have noted, is singular.

   Person refers to the three sets of people or things involved in a conversation or any communication:

   The **first person** is the one speaking (or writing): I, we, myself, etc.

   The **second person** is the one spoken to (or reading): you, yourself, etc.

   The **third person** is the one spoken (or written) **about**: she, he, it, they, etc., and all nouns when you use them in order to speak about people, things, etc.

   The words in column 2 are nouns and third person pronouns. You can therefore put the rule of subject-verb agreement in this way:

   Add an **s** to the verb in the present simple tense when its subject is singular and third person.

6. **A list of two or more nouns or pronouns joined by and is a plural subject:**

   You and Fareeda **look** alike.

   Mr John, Ms Fereira and Ms Ramdeen **take** turns chairing the general meeting.

Present Simple Tense **E3**

7. Look back at the spelling rules shown in C2. When you have to add an s to a verb, the same spelling rules apply.

8. The following verbs remain the same with all subjects – they never take an s ending: can, may, must, shall, will. (See also E18:1.2.)

E3 Practice

1. Make sentences from the substitution table given below.

   Say each sentence aloud before writing it down.

   Return to the table from time to time and make more sentences. You can make over 1,000 sentences from this table.

   Here is how to use a substitution table:

   Take a word or a phrase from each column to make up a sentence, but your sentence must not cross the horizontal line running across columns 1 and 2.

   For example:

   The neighbours prefer the *TNT Mirror*.
   Ayesha and her brother hate Epsom Salts.
   That student takes the easy way out.
   He chooses the national airline.

   You cannot take a word or phrase from above the horizontal line, for example "The neighbours" and put it with a verb from below the line such as "avoids".

   Note that the horizontal line does not run across column 3, so you can use any phrase in column 3 with anything that goes before.

1	2	3
I You We They People The neighbours Ayesha and her brother Drivers	take choose hate prefer avoid	hasty decisions. the North Coast Road. the easy way out. Epsom Salts. *The Gleaner.* difficult assignments. responsibility.
He She Chris The neighbour Ayesha That student The governor My supervisor	takes chooses hates prefers avoids	comic books. a long holiday. adventure stories. the bus. the national airline. *the TNT Mirror.*

2. Supply suitable present simple tense verbs for these sentences:

   (a) Regular exercise _____ you a fit person.

   (b) My children _____ their teeth without toothpaste.

   (c) I _____ a few lines in my diary every night.

   (d) Gloria _____ sweetly at him, but he _____ her.

   (e) That policeman _____ the law.

3. Supply suitable subjects for these sentences:

   (a) As soon as _____ open the window, _____ disappears into the night.

   (b) By the time _____ return, the bush will have covered the house.

   (c) At the end of the day _____ becomes a different person.

   (d) _____ require a great deal of time and effort.

   (e) Everybody can see how much _____ loves this place.

Answers p. 255

E4 THE PRESENT TENSE: CREOLE INFLUENCE

1. CREOLE GRAMMAR

Trinidadian

(a) Them does make too much noise.

(b) Wait till they come.

(c) She know what she doing.

Jamaican

(a) Them make too much noise.

(b) Wait till them come.

(c) She know what she a do.

In sentence (a) the verb shows habitual action (see E2:1.1). In the Trinidad-type Creole, habitual action is shown by placing **does** before the basic verb.

In (b) the present tense verb refers to a future action (see E2:1.2).

In (c) the verb **know** indicates mental action in the present (see E2:3.1).

Note that the verb has the same form whether the subject is singular or plural. In Creole verbs do not change to fit their subjects.

2. **Subject-verb agreement does not exist in Creole.** It is, therefore, an area of English usage that needs our special attention.

When we use the English present simple tense, we may be influenced by Creole usage in different ways:

2.1 Some people use the unmarked form of the verb with all subjects, as in Creole. This produces errors of English:

X *The Roman Catholic Church <u>stand</u> firm on this issue.*
X *He <u>believe</u> that dogs protect a home from burglars.*

2.2 Because we are exposed to English a great deal, we may be aware that an **s** ending is sometimes added to the verb. Yet unless we do plenty of reading, we have some difficulty learning exactly when to add this **s**, because there is no such thing in our first language, Creole. The result is that we are liable to put the **s** in the wrong places:

X *Several factors <u>contributes</u> to road accidents.*
X *These spongy pads <u>enables</u> the cat to move quietly.*

We are perhaps even more liable to make these errors if we think of the rule of subject-verb agreement as

"Singular subject - singular verb
Plural subject - plural verb."

Some people think that this means putting an **s** on the verb for plural subjects. It is the very opposite: a plural subject requires a verb with no **s**.

In any case this simple statement of the rule is misleading. You cannot lump all singular subjects together. (See E3.)

2.3 People who speak the Trinidad-type Creole sometimes carry over the Creole verb pattern into English in a curious way.

In this Creole, the habitual present tense consists of two words, for example, **does walk**. In English it is one word: **walk**, or **walks**. Some people feel very uncomfortable using just one word for this tense. When they use the habitual present tense in English, they feel the need to slide in another word before the verb. Here are some examples of this:

(a) ***What I do on mornings***

Every morning when I get up, I will brush my teeth. Then I will bathe. Next I would put on my clothes and I would eat breakfast. Then my mother would give me money for busfare. My friend would come to meet me and we will go to the bus stop together.

(b) ***The role of a secretary***

A secretary usually types letters for her boss. She normally answers the phone. A secretary always files documents. She will make appointments for her boss. The boss would dictate letters to her and she normally writes them down in shorthand.

These two writers have unconsciously put in another word to take the place of **does**. Writer (a) has put **will** or **would** before each verb. But this means that the verbs are now either in the future tense, or one of the forms discussed in F10, not the habitual present tense. (Some people do this because they are not sure when to put the **s** on the verb: when you put **will** before the verb, there is no **s** ending to contend with!)

Writer (b) uses **will, would, usually, normally,** and **always** with the verb. The repetition of **usually** and **always** is not very good style. Also, **usually** means "most of the time, but not all of the time". Is it an appropriate word to use here?

E4 Practice

1. Some of these sentences contain errors of subject-verb agreement. Identify these errors and correct them.

A. (a) *Some drivers tries in vain to avoid these potholes.*
   (b) *He have his own way of doing things.*
   (c) *The library closes its doors at 5.00 p.m. sharp.*
   (d) *Our teacher give private lessons on Saturdays.*
   (e) *Residents complain about the incessant noise coming from the factory.*

B. (a) *The debate begins on Friday.*
   (b) *You see the harm that drugs does.*
   (c) *Some men consider housework unmanly.*
   (d) *The children has no place to play.*
   (e) *When it rains for days the cisterns and gutters overflows.*

2. Correct the wrong sentences in E4:2.1 and 2.2.

3. Improve the two paragraphs in E4:2.3: **What I do on mornings** and **The role of a secretary**. Remove **will, would, usually, normally** and **always** wherever they occur, and where necessary change the verb to the correct form of the present simple tense.

   Read the corrected paragraphs aloud.

   Answers pp. 255-256

E5 THE VERB *TO BE*

1. We have seen that in the English present simple tense, a verb has two forms: with s and without. (See E1.)

   1.1 The verb **to be** is different. It has three forms in the present simple tense: **am**, **is**, and **are**.

	SUBJECT	VERB
(i)	I	am
(ii)	he/she/it/Nesta/the dog/thunder	is
(iii)	you/we/they/people/the dogs/Carol and Earl	are

The Knots In English

(i) **I** has its own verb – **am**
I am over here.

(ii) All singular third person subjects (see E3:5) take **is**:
Nesta is a reporter.
It is ready.

(iii) With all plural subjects, and **you**, we must use **are**:
The dogs are hungry.
You are on the committee.

1.2 For conversation and informal writing, these verb forms are contracted as follows:

I'm over here.
It's ready.
You're on the committee.

2. CREOLE GRAMMAR

Creole uses only one of the three present tense forms of **to be**: **is**. This form is used with all subjects.

2.1 However, the verb **to be** in the present tense is not widely used in Creole. It is found in only two sentence patterns:

2.1.1 *Trinidadian*: Them is some smartman.

In this sentence **is** joins a subject to a noun complement.

(Basic Jamaican uses **a** for this same purpose: Them a jinnal.)

2.1.2 **Is** also occurs in this Creole pattern which is not found in English:

Is blind he blind.
Is upstairs he gone.

(*Jamaican*: A blind him blind.)

2.2 In English, the verb **to be** is found in these positions:

(a) I am the driver. (Followed by a noun complement.)

(b) Don is crazy. (Followed by an adjective complement.)

(c) The girls are with their mother. (Followed by a preposition phrase.)

> (d) Selma is outside. (Followed by an adverb of place.)
>
> (e) They are asking questions. ⎫ (As auxiliary - followed by a participle.
>
> (f) The yard is swept every day. ⎭ See G5 and H2)
>
> 2.2.1 Pattern (a) is used in Trinidadian Creole, with **is** for all subjects. For patterns (b)–(e), Creole uses the adjective, preposition phrase, adverb of place or present participle as the verb – in present tense sentences:
>
> Don crazy.
>
> Selma deh outside.
>
> (In past tense sentences, **was** or **did** is used:
>
> Don was crazy.
>
> Selma did deh outside.)

Again, the rules are different in Creole. The English use of the verb **to be** does not come "naturally" to Creole speakers. It is something we have to acquire.

E5 Practice

1. (a) Make as many sentences as you can from this substitution table. (See **E3 Practice** 1):

I	am	about to leave for work.
My younger brother		in favour of the change.
Hafeeza		afraid of cats.
The other librarian	is	on the way.
She		very uncomfortable.
He		downstairs.
The young people		still optimistic.
Her daughters		grateful for your assistance.
Three of the students	are	in the kitchen.
They		here.
Sidney and Kwame		unable to take part.
You		

(b) You add more items in the second and third sections of column 1. Make sure that each item agrees with the verb in column 2.

2. Put the correct forms of the verb **to be** (present tense) into the blank spaces:
   (a) The new neighbours _____ Jehovah's Witnesses.
   (b) That supervisor_____ a complete fool.
   (c) You _____ a gifted person.
   (d) Jennifer _____ a Spiritual Baptist.
   (e) I _____ your second cousin.

3. Supply suitable subjects for these sentences. Find at least five different subjects for each sentence, and say each complete sentence aloud. Use different kinds of subjects–names, pronouns, nouns with determiners, and nouns modified by adjectives, by adjective phrases or by adjective clauses, for example:
   _____ are reluctant to take that step.
   George and Angela are reluctant to take that step.
   They are reluctant to take that step.
   The participants are reluctant to take that step.
   Foreign investors are reluctant to take that step.
   People on fixed incomes are reluctant to take that step.
   Women who have children are reluctant to take that step.

A. (a) When _____ is drunk, beware!
   (b) Go and see if _____ are under the house.
   (c) I find that _____ are too expensive.
   (d) The place seems disorganized because _____ is in charge.
   (e) _____ are loveable creatures.

B. (a) I want to know why _____ is in such a terrible state.
   (b) Nowadays _____ are very hard to find.
   (c) _____ is a much-visited tourist attraction.
   (d) At long last _____ is open for business.
   (e) Unfortunately, _____ are only available between the hours of 9.00 a.m. and 5.00 p.m.

4. In some of the following sentences, the verb **to be** does not agree with its subject. Correct this error where it occurs.

Present Simple Tense **E6**

A. (a) *The effects is so gradual that you don't notice.*

(b) *We have to be aware that noise is also an environmental pollutant.*

(c) *Several areas are today without electricity.*

(d) *We are living in a world today where vehicles is a necessity.*

(e) *I, for example, is the result of a mixed marriage.*

B. (a) *The escaped prisoner is still at large.*

(b) *Now that you are in a steady job, you can help to support your children.*

(c) *Your role are to provide the refreshments.*

(d) *Nobody seems to know what the fuss is about.*

(e) *The small space and lack of exercise is bad for the dog's health.*

Answers p. 256

E6 IDENTIFYING THE HEAD WORD

1. When the subject of a sentence stands right before the verb, it is easy enough to make the two of them agree. Quite often, however, people make errors of subject-verb agreement because they do not correctly identify the subject.

1.1 When the subject is a phrase (see B6) one might have some difficulty deciding which word to make the verb agree with.

X (a) *The cost of secondary school texts are exorbitant.*

X (b) *Some raucous men fixing the road outside our house starts work at 6.00 a.m.*

X (c) *A full and detailed report sent to the directors of the firm contain all the necessary information.*

X (d) *Smoking so many cigarettes have its consequences.*

In all of these sentences there are many words coming before the verb, and the writers may have chosen the wrong one to make the verb agree with. Often people assume that the word just before the verb must be the subject.

1.2 When the subject is a phrase, what one has to do is pick out the noun which is the main word or **head** of the phrase. That is the word the verb must agree with.

How do we recognize the head word?

The head word in a noun phrase is the noun (or noun-substitute) which names the thing we are really talking about. The other words in the phrase are determiners and modifiers attached to this word. (See A3, A9.3.1 and B6:4.)

Therefore the **meaning** of what we are saying is our first guide.

In sentence (a) the thing we are calling "exorbitant" is not the school, or the texts, but the cost.

In (b) it is the men we are focusing on. Neither the road nor the house can "start work" at any time at all.

1.3 *The head word in a noun phrase cannot be a possessive noun (D1) or an adjectival noun (D4).*

The head words in these two phrases are in italics:

Joseph's new *job*

the history *books* on the shelf

Joseph's cannot be the head word because it is a possessive noun, and **history** cannot be the head word because here it is in an adjectival role. **Shelf** cannot be it, either, for the respon explained in 1.4 below.

1.4 In identifying the head word, we also have to eliminate any noun which is an object **within the phrase** – the object of either a preposition or a verb form which is part of the phrase. Let us look again at the following phrase:

some raucous men fixing the road outside our house

First of all we know that the head word must be a noun. That eliminates the determiners **some, the** and **our;** the adjective **raucous;** and the preposition **outside**. **Fixing** is a present participle acting as an adjective. (See H1.) We are left with the nouns **men, road** and **house.**

Road cannot be the head because it is the object of the verb form **fixing**.

House cannot be the head because it is the object of the preposition **outside**.

The only noun in this phrase that can be the head is **men**.

1.5 When the subject of a sentence is a phrase, the verb must agree with the head word of that phrase.

The head word is the noun in the phrase which is not possessive, adjectival, or an object within the phrase.

1.6 Remember that the **ing** form of the verb, the present participle, can act as an adjective or as a noun. Study H1 before you do **E6 Practice**.

2. When the subject is a phrase such as the following, one does not look for a head noun:

>   Maritime Services Ltd.
>
>   Trinidad and Tobago
>
>   The United Nations
>
>   Women Working for Social Progress

Each of these phrases is the name of an entity – **one** organization, country or other body. The whole phrase is therefore taken as a singular, third person subject:

>   Maritime Services Ltd **operates** from the port.
>
>   Trinidad and Tobago **produces** oil.

Note that the main words in these phrases begin with capital letters.

3. Nor do we look for a head noun for the verb to agree with when the subject is (a) a subordinate clause (see B6), or (b) a phrase beginning with an infinitive (see A4:3). In this situation, too, we take the whole group of words together to be a singular, third person subject:

>   **How you express your views** makes a difference.
>
>   **To bring these men here** is madness.

4. Sometimes the subject word is separated from its verb by a subordinate clause, and this can also lead to the error of making the verb agree with the wrong word:

>   X *The competition that goes on among networks <u>force</u> them to improve their programmes.*

The subject of this sentence is **competition,** separated from the verb **(to force)** by the subordinate clause **that goes on among networks**. The verb should be **forces**.

E6 Practice

1. Identify the head word in each of the following noun phrases:

A. (a) a full and detailed report given to the directors of the firm.
   (b) your adopting a child
   (c) the temperature in this room
   (d) some very sleek and expensive-looking cars
   (e) children taken out of school

B. (a) the lawyer representing them
   (b) a review of the issues involved
   (c) the roofs of neighbours' houses
   (d) various attempts to overthrow the government
   (e) this year's calypso competition

C. (a) Trinidad and Tobago's balance of payments situation
   (b) public health care facilities
   (c) a large overfed ginger cat with a collar around its neck
   (d) the third building on their right
   (e) clear signs of progress

D. (a) her three-year-old cousin
   (b) women seeking employment
   (c) the governments of Barbados and Guyana
   (d) my grandmother's first daughter
   (e) repainting a house of this size

E. (a) the safety of the strong, old building
   (b) rank-and-file members of the party
   (c) going into the supermarket with a small child
   (d) villages situated deep in the country
   (e) the person driving the car

2. Put the correct present simple tense form of the verb given into the blank slot:

A. (a) The vagrants who roam the city by day _____ in the square at night. (to sleep)
   (b) ALM Antillean Airlines _____ you convenient transfer facilities and even free overnighting. (to offer)
   (c) The smoke from all those factories _____ the air. (to pollute)
   (d) Grenada, Carriacou and Petite Martinique _____ tourists to its shores. (to welcome)
   (e) The discovery of some unmarked graves just outside San Fernando _____ the topic of conversation today all over the country. (to be)

B. (a) Trinidad and Tobago's Water and Sewerage Authority _____ water rates on a quarterly basis. (to collect)
   (b) The burden of housework and childcare still _____ mainly on the shoulders of women. (to fall)

Present Simple Tense **E6**

    (c) Gaily B. and Associates _____ the public to the launching of the band "Zimbabwe". (to invite)

    (d) Villages situated deep in the country _____ the most basic amenities. (to lack)

    (e) Where all this is going to lead us _____ to be seen. (to remain)

C. (a) Every year Women Working for Social Progress _____ events in commemoration of the Day Against Violence to Women. (to organize)

    (b) Sometimes potholes in the road _____ car tyres to blow out. (to cause)

    (c) At election time the rank-and-file members of the party _____ very active. (to become)

    (d) The University of the West Indies _____ a range of degree and diploma programmes. (to offer)

    (e) Spending so many hours in the sun _____ the skin. (to damage)

3. Some of these sentences contain errors of subject-verb agreement. Identify these errors and correct them.

A. (a) *Development for many of the Caribbean countries remains at a standstill.*
    (b) *All the people on board the boat wears life preservers.*
    (c) *The pace of our lives change with age.*
    (d) *The range of programmes produced are indeed limited.*
    (e) *Those clouds gathering in the sky mean rain within the next hour.*

B. (a) *The increase in the number of automobiles also contributes to air pollution.*
    (b) *Workers at this fast food outlet stand for hours on end.*
    (c) *The presence of sufficient military hardware, for example, guns, tanks, missiles, warplanes and a large army of men, is essential in preserving a country's sovereignty.*
    (d) *Children playing games in the street has no regard for safety.*
    (e) *Commissions of enquiry turns out quite often to be a pure waste of time.*

C. (a) *People from the village who witnessed the crime is now afraid to come forward.*
    (b) *The pencils that you found in the drawer belongs to Georgie.*
    (c) *In the Caribbean, nuclear families, where they exist, tend to be part of a wider family network.*
    (d) *The people of this village, because they are poor and uneducated, gets very little attention from the politicians.*
    (e) *Houses which were built before that date face the threat of demolition.*

4. Correct the wrong sentences in E6:1.1.

Answers p. 256

E7 PRESENT TENSE VERBS IN JOINED SENTENCES

Here is another common error:

    X (a) *The leader calls meetings and <u>preside</u> over them.*
    X (b) *Sarah faces great hardship in her life but never <u>complain.</u>*

Each of these is really two sentences joined together:

    (a) The leader calls meetings.
        The leader presides over them.

    (b) Sarah faces great hardship in her life.
        Sarah never complains.

You can see that in each case the two sentences have the same subject. When we join the sentences, therefore, we need not repeat the subject for the second one. The subject of the second sentence is understood.

In this situation many people get the first verb right, but by the time they get to the second verb they may have lost sight of the subject. Because the subject is not placed right next to the second verb, all thoughts of subject-verb agreement go out the window. Remember that many a "sentence" is really sentences or clauses joined together. (See B1 and B6.) We must make sure we recognize all the finite verbs and their subjects.

Some sentences contain two or more verbs attached to one subject. All of those verbs, if they are in the present tense, must agree with that subject.

E7 Practice

1. In each of the following sentences replace the subject in bold type with each of the subjects given, changing the verbs to suit. (NB: In sentence D. you will also need to change the possessive pronoun **her**.)

A. On Saturdays **we** clean the house and do the grocery shopping.

    (a) Henry   (b) the neighbours
    (c) she   (d) the eldest child
    (e) working women.

B. **She** hates cats of any description but tolerates dogs.

    (a) The adults in my home   (b) Our teacher
    (c) Mr Oliver and his wife   (d) This child
    (e) Certain people

C. On Christmas Day **families** wake up early and attend a church service.
- (a) my grandmother
- (b) Rose and her children
- (c) that hypocrite
- (d) the children
- (e) the whole village

D. **Miss Gladys** arrives before daybreak, sets out **her** stock and awaits **her** regular customers.
- (a) The fish vendors
- (b) The man with the pumpkins
- (c) People selling in the Tunapuna market
- (d) George and his partner
- (e) You

E. Before setting out for work **she** feeds and dresses the baby, makes up the other children's lunch-kits and barely manages to drink a cup of coffee.
- (a) you
- (b) one
- (c) Kathleen
- (d) these women
- (e) my aunt

2. Correct the errors of subject-verb agreement in the following sentences:

A. (a) *The doctor stops the treatment or disconnect the life-sustaining system.*
   (b) *We start the aircraft and calls the control tower for clearance.*
   (c) *As a nurse, one encounters or have to deal with people from different backgrounds.*
   (d) *His first point is supported by good evidence but lack proper development.*
   (e) *These unhealthy practices shorten their lives day by day and is a threat to the security of their families.*

B. (a) *The waste material leaks out of the container and enter the soil water thereby poisoning it.*
   (b) *The other child is not able to afford clothes like these, and feel inferior.*
   (c) *It also barks and make other sounds.*
   (d) *The applicant is a resident of St Thomas, is a graduate of a local public school, and wish to pursue a career in nursing or dentistry.*
   (e) *It is here that the individual really matures and become a person.*

Answers pp. 256-257

E8 VERB BEFORE SUBJECT

1. In an English sentence the subject usually comes before the verb. Sometimes, however, this order is inverted (or turned around) so that the verb comes before its subject. This is known as *inversion*.

   Inversion sometimes takes place when a sentence begins with a prepositional phrase, or an adverb of place or direction (showing where or where to):

   (a) High on the hill stand two white houses.

   (b) Upon your shoulders lies a heavy responsibility.

   (c) Here is the glass.

   (d) Here comes your mother.

   (e) Up goes the flag.

   In each of these sentences the verb is underlined twice and the subject once.

   This is another sentence pattern which requires care with subject-verb agreement. If you assume that in every sentence whatever comes before the verb is the subject, then you will produce errors such as these:

   X *High on the hill stands two white houses.*

   X *Upon your shoulders lie a heavy responsibility.*

   In each of these two sentences, the phrase that comes before the verb is a prepositional phrase. A prepositional phrase can only be a **modifier** (see A3 and A5). It cannot be a subject (see B2:2.3).

   Review E6:1. There is no noun in the opening phrase of either sentence which can be the subject of the verb. Both **hill** and **shoulders** are objects of prepositions. Neither can therefore be the subject of a verb.

2. **CREOLE GRAMMAR**

   > The Creole equivalents of sentences (c) and (d) above are:
   >
   > (c) Look the glass. (*Trinidadian*)
   >
   >   See the glass here. (*Jamaican*)
   >
   > (d) Look your mother coming. (*Trinidadian*)
   >
   >   See your mother a come. (*Jamaican*)

3. Be on the look-out for subject-verb inversion, and make sure that the verb agrees with the right word.

E8 Practice

1. Put the correct present simple tense form of the verb given into the blank slot:

A. (a) Uppermost in their minds _____ the question of fundraising. (to be)
   (b) With all these positive results also _____ a negative side effect. (to come)
   (c) Under this bridge _____ the polluted waters of the Tuparo river. (to run)
   (d) Two miles from the police station _____ a healthy field of marijuana. (to grow)
   (e) Among the first to arrive at the bar on evenings _____ the heavy drinkers. (to be)

B. (a) There _____ your last chance for reconciliation. (to go)
   (b) Here _____ the files that you asked for. (to be)
   (c) Out _____ the real story. (to come)
   (d) Here _____ Joan's solution to these problems. (to be)
   (e) There _____ the ruins of our oldest school. (to lie)

Answers p. 257

E9 THERE IS/ARE

1. Here is another case of verb before subject:

   There <u>are</u> some <u>biscuits</u> in the pan.

   The subject is **biscuits** and the verb is **are.**

2. Caribbean people may have a certain amount of difficulty with the expression there + to be because we have a different way of saying this.

   CREOLE GRAMMAR
   > It have some biscuit in the pan.
   > It have a man downstairs.
   > It got water in the gas.
   > It got some fellas here looking for you.
   > Them have a new store in town.

> Them have some wicked people over there.
>
> You can see that Creole does not use the verb **to be** for this kind of sentence. We use **to have** or **to get** with the subject **it** or **them**.

3. When you use the expression there + to be, the subject follows, and the verb to be must agree with that subject.

4. NB: Some Caribbean people think that the English for the Creole expressions it have and them have are it has and they have:

   X *It has* a man downstairs.
   X *They have* some wicked people over there.

   These are *not* Standard English sentences. In Standard English these would be:

   There is a man downstairs.
   There are some wicked people over there.

5. In English the word there can be used with a few other verbs in the same way that it is used with to be. Often it is used with other verbs combined with the infinitive to be:

   There exists an underground route.
   There seem to be two approaches to this question.
   There appears to be a deadlock.

E9 Practice

1. Make sentences from this table. Use **there is** with each of the phrases above the double line, and **there are** with each of the phrases below the double line. Say the sentences aloud.

There is	water in the bottle. one question still to be answered. a fly in the milk. only one way of looking at this. a large crowd of people in that elevator. beer in the fridge. a wide range of products to choose from.
There are	too many people in that elevator. some questions still to be answered. flies in the milk. several ways of looking at this. over twenty products to choose from. two litres of water in the bottle. a few beers in the fridge.

Present Simple Tense **E10**

2. Insert **there is** or **there are** in each blank space, paying attention to subject-verb agreement.

   (a) I agree that _____ certain things which must be kept secret.

   (b) _____ children in need of special attention.

   (c) Even in the churches _____ discrimination against women.

   (d) It seems that _____ some differences of opinion which must be resolved.

   (e) _____ one major flaw in all these plans.

3. Put the correct present simple tense form of the verb given with each sentence into the blank slot.

   (a) There _____ to be queries about the minister's health. (to continue)

   (b) The doctors say that there _____ a 20% chance of recovery. (to remain)

   (c) Fortunately for the young people of today, there _____ other outlets for their energy. (to exist)

   (d) There _____ to be a breakdown in the postal services. (to appear)

   (e) In every person's life there _____ a time when a difficult choice must be made. (to come)

   Answers p. 257

E10 RELATIVE PRONOUN AS SUBJECT

1. Review B6:2 and 3.

In each of the following sentences there is a subordinate clause which modifies a noun or a pronoun:

(a) He has to make decisions **that affect other people's lives**.

(b) This is a pothole **which causes accidents**.

(c) You **who are about to take on this task** must be aware of the responsibility involved.

The subjects of these subordinate clauses are (a) **that,** (b) **which** and (c) **who**. These words are known as **relative pronouns.** Each of them represents the noun or pronoun to which the clause refers. To demonstrate this, we could break down the sentences as follows:

(a) He has to make decisions.   The decisions affect other people's lives.

(b) This is a pothole.   The pothole causes accidents.

(c) You must be aware of the responsibility involved.   You are about to take on this task.

2. A relative pronoun has the same number and person as the noun or pronoun which it represents.

But you cannot tell by looking at a relative pronoun what number or person it is. Relative pronouns remain the same whether they are singular or plural, first, second or third person.

Therefore, when a relative pronoun is the subject of a present tense verb, you have to pay special attention to subject-verb agreement. The verb must agree with the word which the relative pronoun represents.

In sentence (a), **that** represents **decisions. That** is therefore plural, and the verb **to affect** has no **s** ending.

In sentence (b), **which** represents **pothole.** Therefore the verb **to cause** has an **s** ending to agree with **pothole.**

In sentence (c), **who** represents **you.** The present tense form of the verb **to be** that goes with **you** is **are.**

Watch out for present tense verbs in clauses which have a relative pronoun as their subject, and avoid errors such as this:

X Where are the policemen who <u>directs</u> traffic at this intersection?

Correct this sentence.

3. NB: A relative pronoun is not always the subject of the clause which it introduces. Often the clause has its own subject, and the verb must agree with that word:

(a) You need to monitor the television programmes **that your child watches.**

(b) The scenes **which the audience appreciates the most** are likely to be censored.

(c) Alicia is surrounded by people **whom she trusts.**

3.1 In these sentences the relative pronoun is the **object** of the subordinate clause, even though it appears at the beginning of the clause.

In (a) **that** represents **programmes:**
Your child watches programmes.

In (b) **which** represents **the scenes:**
The audience appreciates the scenes...

In (c) **whom** represents **people:**
Alicia trusts people.

3.2 **Whom** (in sentence (c) is the object form of **who.** In less formal language **who** can be used in the same slot:

Alicia is surrounded by people who she trusts.

3.3 In these sentences, too, the relative pronoun can be left out:

(a) You need to monitor the television programmes your child watches.

(b) The scenes the audience appreciates the most are likely to be censored.

(c) Alicia is surrounded by people she trusts.

E10 Practice

1. Take each clause on the left and join it to each of the clauses on the right **which can correctly be joined to it.**

    Say the new sentences aloud before writing them down. Each table can yield 25 correct sentences.

A.

	who works for the Parks Oil Co.
	who have nothing to lose.
(a) These are the people	who live in the housing settlement.
(b) We would like to speak with a Mrs Hector	who speaks French.
	who work the hardest.
(c) These words are especially addressed to you	who belongs to the National Party.
	who donate blood regularly.
(d) He has sent the letter to a cousin	who fear the police.
(e) The last caller is someone	who lives in the USA.
	who keeps a large German Shepherd dog.

B.

	which create conflict.
	which are not relevant to the discussion.
(a) They are not interested in anything	which invites confrontation.
(b) Refrain from making remarks	which offend certain groups.
(c) This is the part	which is potentially disruptive.
(d) Your articles contain statements	which requires concentration.
(e) He is again putting forward theories	which have no basis.
	which appears to be difficult.
	which is not convincing.
	which make no sense.

C.

	that offer a viable alternative.
	that seems feasible.
	that really impress me.
(a) We have received a proposal	that are both innovative and workable.
(b) I have not yet heard any suggestions	that solves the problems identified.
(c) The government is about to implement certain policies	that promise to enhance the image of the country.
(d) I hope that this committee will come up with a long-term plan	that takes all these issues into consideration.
(e) A women's organization is embarking upon a project	that has the potential to succeed.
	that give us hope for the improvement of life in the community.
	that makes more sense than previous ones of its kind.

2. Some of these sentences contain errors of subject-verb agreement. Correct these errors.

   (a) *It has resulted in changes which greatly affects women.*

   (b) *The panel discussion is open to all members of the public who is interested in this issue.*

(c) *They are not capable of dealing with the problems that confront us.*
(d) *We are looking for the lady who run the shoe store.*
(e) *A "solution" which creates new problems cannot really be seen as a solution.*

Answers pp. 257-258

E11 SUBJECTS WITH QUANTITY EXPRESSIONS

1. Review C8 and C9.

When the subject of a sentence involves a quantity expression, problems of subject-verb agreement may arise. When are these subjects singular, and when are they plural?

2. Singular subjects

All of the following are singular, third-person subjects. They call for an **s** on the verb.

2.1 *Uncountable nouns with quantity expressions*

Uncountable nouns are always singular (unless they are being used countably – see C5:4). Whatever the quantity expression you use with an uncountable noun, you can only be referring to one thing.

A phrase made up of words like the following plus an **uncountable noun** is a singular subject:

all (of)	a little (of)	no
any (of)	a lot of	none of
enough (of)	more (of)	plenty (of)
half (of)	most (of)	the rest of
less (of)	much (of)	some (of)

For example:

No alcohol **enters** this house.
The rest of the information **is** confidential.
Some equipment **requires** very careful handling.

(In Section 3.1 below you will see that most of these same quantity expressions, when used with plural nouns, give you phrases that are plural.)

2.2 *Phrases with quantity expressions meaning "one":*

When one of the following expressions is placed before a noun or pronoun, the phrase that is formed is singular:

another (of), each (of), every, one (of)

Some of these expressions are used with plural nouns, or a list of nouns. In such cases the phrase is still singular:

>Every man, woman and child **helps** with the clearing of the land.
>
>Another storm **seems** imminent.
>
>Each of you **has** a legitimate claim.
>
>One of her sons **lives** downstairs.

2.3 *Pronouns meaning "one"*

All of the following are singular pronouns:

>anyone, anything, everybody, everyone, nobody, none, one.

When one of these is the subject of a present tense verb, that verb must have an **s** ending:

>One **needs** to take a careful look at this new development.
>
>Everybody **wants** to reap the benefits, but nobody **wants** to make the sacrifice.

3. Plural subjects

3.1 When the quantity expressions below are used with plural nouns (see C8) or pronouns, the phrases formed are plural:

all (of)	(a) few (of)	many (of)	plenty (of)
any (of)	fewer (of)	more (of)	the rest of
both (of)	half (of)	most (of)	several (of)
a couple of	a lot of	no	some (of)
enough (of)	the majority of	a number of	

For example:

>Few of the children **have** all the required textbooks.
>
>Some schools **forbid** the wearing of jewelry.
>
>No buses **run** along this road.

3.2 NB: There is some uncertainty about whether "a number of..." is singular or plural.

It is quite acceptable to treat "a number of..." as a plural subject. Technically, yes, "number" is a singular word, and when a singular word is the head word of a phrase (see E6) that phrase is singular. But in normal English usage "a number of" with a plural noun is treated as a plural phrase. The same applies to some other singular quantity words – "a couple", "a few", "a lot" and "the majority":

>A number of obstacles **stand** in the way.
>The majority of us **are** serious, hard-working people.

(In all other situations the word "number" **is** singular:

>The number of vagrants **increases** from day to day.
>Number 345 **wins** the trophy.)

4. Either and neither

4.1 When **either** and **neither** are used to refer to singular nouns or pronouns, the phrases formed are singular:

>Either party **runs** the risk of legal action.
>Neither of these two options **seems** feasible.

4.2 **Either** and **neither** are most often used with **or** and **nor** respectively:

>Either June or her brother **keeps** the key.
>Neither the radio nor the television set **works** properly.

In each of these two sentences, the subject is only one thing, not two. Nouns joined by **or** or **nor** are alternatives.

In the first sentence, for example, we can take "June" to be the subject, or, we can think of "her brother" as the subject – not both of them.

Compare the following:

>June and her brother **keep** the key.
>The radio and the television set **are** out of order.

Here the same two nouns are joined by **and.** "June" and "her brother" are added together to make up a plural subject.

4.3 Singular nouns and pronouns joined by **or** or **nor** are singular subjects, even when they are part of a longer list:

>Neither the house, the land, the furniture nor the livestock **is** up for sale.

In the sentences given here, **either...or** and **neither...nor** are used with singular nouns only. Therefore subject-verb agreement is straightforward.

4.4 **Either** and **neither** can also be used with plurals. When only plural nouns are involved, subject-verb agreement is also straightforward.

> Either rats or cockroaches **are** responsible for this.
> Neither the radios nor the television sets **work** properly.

4.5 However, in some sentences **either** and **neither** are used with a mixture of singular and plural nouns. When such a construction is the subject of a sentence, the verb usually agrees with the noun (or pronoun) nearest to it:

> Either June or her brothers **keep** the key.

> Neither the radios nor the television set **works** properly.

5. Quantity expressions as pronouns

5.1 Quantity expressions can be either adjectives or pronouns:

> (a) Most banks offer this service.

> (b) Most of the banks offer this service.

In (a) **most** is an adjective modifying **banks.**

In (b) **most** is a pronoun referring to **banks** which is plural. **Most** is therefore a plural subject in this sentence.

Compare the following:

> (c) Most of the land belongs to her grandmother.

Here **most** is a pronoun referring to something singular: **land.** (See 2.1 above.) Therefore the verb has an **s** ending to agree with it.

5.2 Sometimes a quantity expression stands on its own as a pronoun. It refers to a noun which is not stated. The noun is understood:

> (d) Most of the garbage is biodegradable, but **some** is not.

In this sentence, **some** is a singular subject requiring the verb form **is,** because **some** refers to the singular noun **garbage.**

Compare the following:

> (e) Most of the shareholders are in favour of the merger, but **some** are still doubtful.

Here **some** is plural, because it refers to **shareholders.** Therefore the form of the verb that agrees with it is **are.**

E11 Practice

1. Supply the correct form of the verb **to be** (**is** or **are**):

A. (a) A number of items _____ on display.

   (b) Each of the sub-themes _____ equally important.

   (c) After a party there _____ a lot of garbage everywhere.

   (d) There _____ a few technical terms that need to be defined.

   (e) Many are called, but few _____ chosen.

B. (a) There _____ some variation in their income levels.

   (b) Not all agricultural machinery _____ as efficient as this.

   (c) Some of your suggestions _____ not very practical.

   (d) There _____ enough people here to make up a quorum.

   (e) Either UNESCO or the Ministry of Women's Affairs _____ responsible for that project.

2. In each of the following sentences replace the phrase in bold type with each of the phrases given, changing the relevant verb to suit.

   For example:

   Some **equipment** requires very careful handling.

   (a) Some gadgets...

   Some gadgets require very careful handling.

A. **Each speaker** has a different style.

   (a) Each of the speakers...

   (b) Some of the speakers...

   (c) The rest of the speakers...

   (d) Every speaker...

   (e) One of the speakers...

B. **Some of the schools** receive government funding.

   (a) No private school...

   (b) Few pre-primary schools...

   (c) Most of the schools...

(d) All schools...

(e) Every school in this district...

C. **All of the chairs** fit into one room.

(a) All of the furniture...

(b) All of the people...

(c) Most of the equipment...

(d) Much of the merchandise...

(e) About half of the crates...

D. They have already removed **some of the appliances** that belong to the company.

(a) some of the machines...

(b) some of the machinery...

(c) some equipment...

(d) a few pieces of equipment...

(e) most of the stock...

E. Clearly **most of you** know the whole story.

(a) everybody...

(b) the majority of us...

(c) nobody...

(d) some people...

(e) neither Yvonne nor Mr Cuffie...

Answers p. 258

E12 VERBS ENDING WITH A SOUND LIKE *S*

Look back at C10.

When verbs end with a sound like **s** a similar problem can arise. Some people do not bother to add the **s** for agreement:

X (a) *The company possess the right equipment for the job.*

X (b) *He experience the same problem whenever he travels by air.*

The **s** sound at the end of **possess** and **experience** is part of the word. We still need to add **s** to make them agree with their subjects:

> The company **possesses**...
>
> He **experiences**...

E12 Practice

Put the correct present simple tense form of the verb into the blank slot:
- (a) If she _____ this opportunity nobody will take her seriously. (to waste)
- (b) Problems such as these _____ wherever there is poverty. (to exist).
- (c) Your presence here _____ that you have not lost interest. (to suggest).
- (d) Every year on Independence Day the Prime Minister _____ the nation on radio and television. (to address)
- (e) The mistakes of today _____ you to be more careful in the future. (to force)

Answers p. 258

E13 UNCHANGEABLE NOUN AS SUBJECT

Look back at C11.

When one of these nouns is the subject of a present tense verb, there can be problems of agreement.

Is the subject singular, or is it plural?

Some unchangeable nouns are always to be treated as singular, some are always to be treated as plural, and others can be singular or plural depending on meaning:

Always Singular	*Always Plural*	*Singular/Plural*
aerobics	glasses	aircraft
apparel	pants	offspring
baggage	scissors	personnel
economics	spectacles	
equipment		

Always Singular cont.   ***Always Plural cont.***   ***Singular/Plural cont.***

furniture
gravel
gymnastics
jargon
luggage
mathematics
news
politics
print

Here are two sentences with subjects from the first two columns:

> When the news breaks, there will be a riot.
> Those pants need ironing.

Words like **aircraft** and **offspring** are singular subjects if they refer to one item, and plural when they refer to more than one:

> This device ensures that the aircraft makes a smooth landing.
> Aircraft remain on the ground when there is a hurricane watch.

> My colleague's offspring Shawn behaves exactly like his progenitor.
> That man's offspring are everywhere.

Personnel is singular when we want to convey the idea of one body or group of people, and plural if we are thinking of "personnel" as a number of individuals:

> Your personnel has to be trained.
> The company's personnel are pleasant and efficient.

E13 Practice

1. Make sentences from these substitution tables.

A.

The	equipment		in the warehouse.
Your	furniture		up for sale.
All the	gravel	is	under the scrutiny of the police.
Some	baggage		already on its way.
Somebody's	luggage		about to be auctioned off.

B.

Politics		not my cup of tea.
Mathematics		a very interesting pursuit.
Economics	is	not as difficult as it seems.
Gymnastics		for people who have the aptitude for it.
Aerobics		fascinating to the novice.

2. Put the correct present simple tense form of the verb given in the blank slot.

(a) Too much jargon _____ the reader. (to confuse)

(b Personnel who _____ the hardest are rewarded accordingly. (to work)

(c) Her new spectacles _____ her look different. (to make)

(d) Have we got any scissors that actually _____? (to cut)

(e) The print _____ so fine that you need a magnifying glass to read it. (to be)

Answers p. 259

E14 QUESTION FORM OF THE PRESENT TENSE

1. **CREOLE GRAMMAR**

STATEMENT	QUESTION
Trinidadian	
You does walk to school.	You does walk to school?
The child does walk to school.	The child does walk to school?
The children does walk to school.	The children does walk to school?
Jamaican	
You walk to school.	You walk to school?
The pickney him walk to school.	The pickney him walk to school?
The pickney-dem walk to school.	The pickney-dem walk to school?

All of these sentences are in the present tense.

One column contains statements, and the other contains the equivalent questions.

Take note of the following:

1.1 The question in Creole has the same structure as the statement. Then how can we tell the difference? Read each statement and its question form aloud. You will notice that the question has a different intonation or "tune" which goes up at the end. Everything else is the same.

1.2 As we have already noted (see E4) the verb remains the same, whatever the subject.

2. The question (or "interrogative") form is yet another rule of Creole that we tend to carry over into English.

   2.1 In writing English, Caribbean people sometimes place a question mark at the end of a statement to turn it into a question; or, in speaking, we might use the statement form to pose a question, simply using the intonation of a question. This is not how questions are normally formed in English.

   2.2 In English, statements are **sometimes** used as questions. In an informal conversation, a speaker might say:

   "You remember that bar we used to hang out in?"

   Here the speaker is not really seeking information, for she/he is fairly sure that the other person remembers the bar. So the sentence *is* more like a statement than a real question. It is a confirmation rather than an enquiry.

Read these dialogues:

(a) *Ms Hackett:* The school is three miles from the village, but these children walk to school.

   Mr Blackett: **These children walk to school?** Incredible!

(b) *Teacher:* Garvin, where does wheat come from?

   Garvin: Miss, wheat comes from Barbados, Miss.

   Teacher: **Wheat comes from Barbados?** Garvin, you are not paying attention!

The sentences in bold type are spoken as questions. But the people saying them are not really seeking information. They already know the answers to their "questions". So these are not really questions. They are more like exclamations.

Now let us look at how true questions are formed in English.

3.

Statement	Question
You **walk** to school.	**Do** you **walk** to school?
The child **walks** to school.	**Does** the child **walk** to school?
The children **walk** to school.	**Do** the children **walk** to school?

Note the following three points:

3.1 In the English question form the verb splits into two parts – auxiliary and main verb. The main verb takes the form of the infinitive without **to**. (See A4:3.)

   walk becomes **do + walk**

   walks becomes **does + walk**

3.2 The subject of the sentence comes after the auxiliary verb. It gets sandwiched between the two parts of the verb.

3.3 The *auxiliary verb "to do" agrees with the subject;* the second part, or main verb, does not.

   The main verb here is an infinitive and *remains the same, whatever the subject.* (See E18:1.)

4. **Look at the following sentences:**

   (a) They always walk to school.
   (b) Do they always walk to school?

(c) Jean sometimes visits her relatives in the country.
(d) Does Jean sometimes visit her relatives in the country?

Note the position of the adverbs **always** and **sometimes.**

There are certain adverbs which, in a statement, may come before the verb, as in sentences (a) and (c) above. In the question form of such sentences, the adverb goes before the main verb, as in sentences (b) and (d).

E14 Practice

1. Make sentences from these substitution tables.

A.

Does	the chairperson everybody here Gary Your assistant Ma	remember the incident? agree with what I'm saying? work hard? object to the noise? like Jamaican music?
Do	most of the men your sisters the members of the committee Gary and his friends some of you	earn enough money to live on? have access to a telephone? read the newspapers? smoke? know about this?

B.

Does	Aunty June Uncle Malcolm she he the tenant	ever normally always	watch soap operas on TV? boil drinking water? bathe in the river? allow the dogs inside? make overseas calls during the day?
Do	you any of these people they your cousins Sandra's grandparents	sometimes occasionally frequently usually	wear dark glasses? walk around the savannah? have premonitions which come true? listen to that radio station? give money to beggars?

Present Simple Tense **E14**

C.

Why When Where How	does	Keith your cousin she this youngster Betty	smoke all those cigarettes? pick up such habits? commit the alleged offences? collect so much junk? peddle drugs?
	do	you they these people your brothers the teenagers	associate with those unsavoury characters? hide the best of the mangoes?

2. Convert the following statements into questions:

A. (a) You agree with everything he says.
   (b) Ms Ramdeen chairs the general meeting.
   (c) The candidates understand what is required of them.
   (d) She wants one of those.
   (e) Michael and his sister sing in the choir.

B. (a) The fish-processing company employs people living in the area.
   (b) Female members participate equally at all levels of the organization.
   (c) Social workers visit the home on a regular basis.
   (d) Each student chooses a different topic.
   (e) Soap operas appeal to all kinds of people.

C. (a) The temperature in this room suits everybody.
   (b) Rank-and-file members of the party support this decision.
   (c) Public health care facilities stay open on weekends.
   (d) The lawyer representing them knows where they are.
   (e) The person driving the car has a driver's permit.

Answers p. 259

E15 NEGATIVE FORM OF THE PRESENT SIMPLE TENSE

1.

A	B
I **walk** to school.	(a) I **do not walk** to school. (b) I **don't walk** to school.
The child **walks** to school.	(a) The child **does not walk** to school. (b) The child **doesn't** walk to school.
The children **walk** to school.	(a) The children **do not** walk to school. (b) The children **don't walk** to school.

The sentences in column A are **affirmative** (or positive) statements, and those in column B are **negative** statements.

As happens with the question form (see E14:3) the verb splits in two for the negative form: auxiliary **to do** and main verb in the infinitive. **Not** is placed after the auxiliary. Here again the auxiliary agrees with the subject and the main verb remains the same with all subjects.

In column B, sentences (a) and (b) mean the same, but (b) is the form more likely to be used in conversation and informal writing. Form (b) is the contraction, or shortened form. The full form (a) is used in formal writing. It is only used in conversation if we want to emphasize the "not".

2. AVOID THESE ERRORS

2.1 *Spelling*

Please note carefully how the negative forms of verbs are written:

2.1.1 When you write the full form of the negative, do not join the auxiliary to **not**. These are incorrect:

    X *donot*   X *doesnot*

Each of these must be written as two separate words:

    do not   does not

It is only when **not** is contracted, or shortened, that it is joined to the auxiliary:

    don't   doesn't

2.1.2 Some people have a problem with the spelling of **doesn't**. They write:

    X *dosen't*

Check your spelling. The word **doesn't** is made up of three parts:

the verb **do**

+

es ending for subject-verb agreement

+

the shortened form of **not: n't**

2.2 Punctuation

When using the contracted form, do not forget to put in the apostrophe, and do not put it in the wrong place.

These are incorrect:

    X   *dont*   *do'nt*   *dont'*   *does'nt*

In contractions, the purpose of the apostrophe is to show where a letter or letters are missing. Here the missing letter is the **o** in **not**, so the apostrophe belongs between **n** and **t**:

    don't   Doesn't

3. CREOLE GRAMMAR

> 3.1 In the Trinidad-type Creole, speakers use forms of **doesn't** and **don't** to make verbs negative; but it is not subject-verb agreement that determines which one is used. The rule tends to be that **doesn't** is used for the present habitual tense (see E2:1.1) with verbs of physical action (A. below), while **don't** is used with verbs of mental action (B. below, and see E2:3.1):
>
> A. I **doesn't** eat fish.
>   Craig **doesn't** interfere with nobody.
>   They **doesn't** drive safe on that road.
>
> B. I **don't** like that fella face at all.
>   Craig **don't** care if Good Friday fall on Ash Wednesday.
>   They **don't** know what they doing.

> 3.2 However, with verbs of mental action the negative marker more likely to be used is **eh**:
>
>> I **eh** like that fella face at all.
>>
>> Craig **eh** care if Good Friday fall on Ash Wednesday.
>>
>> They **eh** know what they doing.
>
> (When **eh** is used with a verb of physical action, that verb cannot be described as "present tense". (See F6:2 and G3:3.) The Creole "He **eh** bathe the dog" corresponds more or less to the English present perfect "He hasn't bathed the dog".)
>
> 3.3 The Jamaican-type Creole uses **no** before the verb to make it negative:
>
>> Me **no** drink no rum.
>>
>> Him **no** favour fe him mother.
>>
>> Them **no** know nothing.
>
> As with **eh** in Trinidadian Creole, **don't** with a verb of physical action is not usually a present tense verb phrase. "Him **don't** come" is closer to the English present perfect (see G3): "He hasn't come."

4. Creole uses forms of doesn't and don't in ways that are different from English. Apart from the differences in meaning, there is the question of subject-verb agreement.

Remember that in English the choice between **doesn't** and **don't** depends on what the subject is. In English these sentences are incorrect:

> X The caretaker <u>don't</u> know where the key is.
>
> X Hindu people <u>doesn't</u> eat beef.

The correct English forms are:

> The caretaker doesn't know where the key is.
>
> Hindu people don't eat beef.

E15 Practice

1. Make sentences from this substitution table.

This The age of the candidate What you think about politicians The person's race His country of origin	does not doesn't	matter. make a difference. interest anyone. bear any relevance to the discussion.
These things A person's religious beliefs Political affiliations Previous agreements Age and experience	do not don't	concern us. influence our assessment. count. change the price of barley.

2. Make the following sentences negative by changing the verb in bold type, using the full and contracted forms. For example:

   Social workers **visit** the home on a regular basis.
   Social workers do not visit the home on a regular basis.
   Social workers don't visit the home on a regular basis.

A. (a) You **agree** with everything he says.

   (b) Ms Ramdeen **chairs** the general meeting.

   (c) The candidates **understand** what is required of them.

   (d) She **wants** one of those.

   (e) Michael and his sister **sing** in the choir.

B. (a) The temperature in this room **suits** everybody.

   (b) Rank-and-file members of the party **support** this decision.

   (c) Public health care facilities **stay** open on weekends.

   (d) The lawyer representing them **knows** where they are.

   (e) The person driving the car **has** a driver's permit.

3. Put the negative present simple tense form of the verb given into the blank slot. Give the full and contracted forms for each. For example:

His parents _____ him to stay out late. (to allow)

His parents do not allow him to stay out late.

His parents don't allow him to stay out late.

A. (a) People in this line of work _____ a lot of money. (to make)

(b) The bus that plies the Sangre Grande route _____ the terminus on time. (to leave)

(c) I most certainly _____ women. (to abuse)

(d) Your nostalgic stories about "the good old days" _____ anybody. (to convince)

(e) The shop in the village _____ a liquor licence. (to have)

B. (a) These bad roads _____ a good impression of the place. (to give)

(b) The report you have submitted _____ enough light on the circumstances surrounding this incident. (to shed)

(c) The contract under which we are operating at present _____ beyond December 31st. (to extend)

(d) It is obvious that you _____ to cooperate. (to intend)

(e) Durham, Pierre and Co. Ltd._____ responsibility for the safety of personal property left in this car park. (to accept).

Answers pp. 259-260

E16 DOUBLE NEGATIVES

THE QUESTION OF DOUBLE NEGATIVES IS PRESENTED HERE WITH THE PRESENT SIMPLE TENSE. PLEASE BEAR IN MIND, HOWEVER, THAT THIS DISCUSSION APPLIES TO ALL TENSES, NOT ONLY THE PRESENT SIMPLE.

1. **CREOLE GRAMMAR**

Trinidadian

(a) I don't[1] want none[2].

(b) The children and them don't[1] know nothing[2].

(c) Mr Nathan doesn't[1] put no[2] salt in he food.

(d) Nobody[1] here doesn't[2] smoke no[3] weed.

> *Jamaican*
> (a) Me no[1] want none[2].
> (b) The pickney them no[1] know nothing[2].
> (c) Mr Nathan no[1] put no[2] salt inna fe him food.
> (d) Nobody[1] here no[2] smoke no[3] weed.
>
> Creole is one of those languages which use more than one negative marker at a time – two, and sometimes more. In sentences (a), (b) and (c), the verb is negative and so is the object. In sentence (d), subject, verb and object are all negative.
>
> This cannot be done in English.

2. In English the sentences given above would be:

(a) I don't want any.

(b) The children don't know anything.

(d) Mr Nathan doesn't put (any) salt in his food.

(d) Nobody here smokes (any) weed.

2.1 In English a negative sentence can only have one negative marker. In the English sentences (a) – (c) above, the verb is negative, and so no other part of the sentence is marked negative. In sentence (d) the subject alone is negative.

2.2 You can, however, deliberately use a double negative to make a *positive* statement:

Nobody here doesn't have a problem.
(MEANING: Everybody here has a problem.)

We don't want to see no parents at PTA meetings.
(MEANING: We want to see parents at PTA meetings.)

Remember that in English if you want a sentence to be negative, you can normally only make one part of it negative – subject, verb, object or complement.

3. Examine these patterns:

(a) They want **some** tea.

(b) They don't want **any** tea.

(a) He gives his brother **some**.

(b) He doesn't give his brother **any**.

(a) I see **some**body coming up.

(b) I don't see **any**body coming up.

(a) We add **some**thing to the water.

(b) We don't add **any**thing to the water.

3.1 The (a) sentences are positive, and in each of them the word **some** appears in the object. But in the (b) sentences the verb is marked negative, and there **some** becomes **any**.

3.2 In some sentences with a negative verb, **any** with the object is optional. It may be used for emphasis:

> Mr Nathan doesn't put salt in his food.
> Mr Nathan doesn't put any salt in his food.
>
> Nobody here smokes weed.
> Nobody here smokes any weed.

3.3 Adverbs such as **never**, **hardly**, **rarely**, **scarcely** and **seldom** with the verb have the same effect as negative markers:

He never has **any** money.

In these discussions Michael rarely finds **any**thing to say.

The eldest boy seldom gets into **any** trouble.

4. Here is another way of making this kind of sentence negative:

(a) They don't want any tea.

(b) They want **no** tea.

(a) He doesn't give his brother any.

(b) He gives his brother **none**.

(a) I don't see anybody coming up.

(b) I see **no**body coming up.

(a) We don't add anything to the water.

(b) We add **no**thing to the water.

In (b) the negative marker shifts from the verb to the object, where **any** is replaced by **no**. This way of making a negative statement is more emphatic than the other. People sometimes use this version if they are arguing, or scolding, or simply being dramatic.

Remember that the problem of double negatives crops up with all tenses, not only the present simple. (See, for example, F6:3.1.)

E16 Practice

1. Make the following sentences negative by (a) making the verb negative, then (b) making the object negative. Give the full and contracted forms of the negative verb. For example:

    He has credentials.

    (a) He does not have credentials (OR any credentials).
    He doesn't have credentials (OR any credentials).

    (b) He has no credentials.

A. (a) The sugar estate pays its workers a bonus at the end of the year.
   (b) These young people have plans for the future.
   (c) Mr Henry needs help with filling out his income tax forms.
   (d) Health centres handle major ailments.
   (e) Government provides support for the handicapped.

B. (a) These figures give us some indication of future trends.
   (b) Paula knows somebody in Port-of-Spain.
   (c) My brothers do some of the housework.
   (d) Residents of this area contribute something towards the maintenance of community facilities.
   (e) Brian keeps some for himself.

2. Correct these sentences:
   (a) *No bus doesn't pass here.*
   (b) *The people behind the desk don't care about nobody.*
   (c) *That company never observes no safety precautions.*
   (d) *Nobody named "Oliver" doesn't live at this address.*
   (e) *When you get money you hardly put aside none.*

Answers pp. 260-261

E17 PRESENT SIMPLE TENSE: NEGATIVE QUESTIONS

1.
   Doesn't the school bus pass near your house?
   Don't I always tell you the truth?
   Don't the children walk to school?

   These are all negative questions. A negative question in English usually expects the answer "Yes".

   What is given above is the contracted form of these sentences. The full form is used only in *very* formal speech or writing, for emphasis:

   Does the school bus not pass near your house?
   Do I not always tell you the truth?
   Do the children not walk to school?

   Since both the English negative form and the English question form are foreign to Creole, negative questions present a certain amount of difficulty.

2. **CREOLE GRAMMAR**

   How do we form negative questions in Creole? There are two ways:

   2.1 The negative sentence is spoken as a question:

   Trinidadian

   The school bus doesn't pass near by your house?
   I doesn't always tell you the truth?
   The children doesn't walk to school?

   Jamaican

   The school bus no pass near fe you house?
   Me no always tell you the truth?
   The pickney-them no walk to school?

   OR

   2.2 A negative word is placed before the question (which in Creole has the same form as a statement):

   Trinidadian

   Ain't the school bus does pass near your house?
   Ain't I does always tell you the truth?
   Ain't the children does walk to school?

   Jamaican

   Don't the school bus pass near fe you house?
   Don't me always tell you the truth?
   Don't the pickney-them walk to school?

3. English negative questions in the present tense require subject-verb agreement. The pattern of the sentence is:

Doesn't or **Don't** - SUBJECT - INFINITIVE FORM OF VERB

E17 Practice

1. Make sentences from this substitution table:

Doesn't	the chairperson	remember the incident?
	everybody here	agree with what I'm saying?
	Gary	work hard?
	your assistant	object to the noise?
	Ma	like Jamaican music?
Don't	most of the men	earn enough money to live on?
	your sisters	have access to a telephone?
	the members of the committee	read the newspapers?
	Gary and his friends	smoke?
	some of you	know about this?

2. Convert each of these sentences to a negative question (contracted form):

A. (a) All of our members live in LaGrange or in communities nearby.

   (b) Mr Barnes controls everything.

   (c) Government ministries owe large sums of money to the Water and Sewerage Authority.

   (d) Sylvester operates a bar on weekends.

   (e) Ms Ramdeen chairs the general meeting.

B. (a) His latest calypso sounds really good.

   (b) They use various oils and perfumes in their ceremonies.

   (c) She works in the garden on weekends.

   (d) Exams begin in two weeks' time.

   (e) You agree with that suggestion.

C. (a) Michael and his sister sing in the church choir.

   (b) The candidates understand what is required of them.

(c) The person driving the car has a driver's permit.

(d) Social workers visit the home on a regular basis.

(e) The fish processing company employs people living in the area.

Answers p. 261

E18 WHERE NOT TO PUT THE *S*

1. The Infinitive

See A4:3.

1.1. When the verb splits into two for questions or for the negative form, people can be confused about subject-verb agreement. Mistakes like these are frequently made:

> X *Why do the company adopts this policy?*
> X *Carla does not has any excuse.*

When the verb consists of more than one word, only the first word must agree with the subject.

In the question form and the negative, the verb consists of two words. The first is an auxiliary. The second is an infinitive. The infinitive **never changes to agree with the subject.** It is the auxiliary verb which changes:

> Why **does** the company **adopt** this policy?
> Why **do** they **adopt** this policy?

> Carla **does** not **have** any excuse.
> You **do** not **have** any excuse.

1.2 Look at these sentences:

> Garvin **can make** good roti.
> You **must keep** the room tidy.
> She **may find** it difficult to leave.

In each of these sentences the verb phrase (in bold type) is made up of an auxiliary and an infinitive. **Can, must** and **may** belong to a special category of verbs known as modal auxiliaries or modals. These are used in the same way as the auxiliary **do/does** (See E14:3 and E15):

Question: Can Garvin make good roti?
Negative: Garvin cannot/can't make good roti.

There is one major difference, however: modal auxiliaries do not change to agree with the subject. They have no form ending in **s**.

Yet people who know the rule of subject-verb agreement may feel that there **has** to be an **s** on the verb somewhere if the subject is third person singular. Therefore when the verb has a modal auxiliary (which never takes an **s** ending) some people seek to solve the "problem" by putting an **s** on the second part of the verb:

X *Garvin can <u>makes</u> very good roti.*

This is wrong, of course, because **make** in this sentence is an infinitive, and you do not put endings on infinitives.

NB: Unlike **do** and **does,** the auxiliary **can** is joined to not: **cannot.**

1.3 Here is another use of the infinitive:

> I **watch** the bottle **fall** to the floor.
> He **feels** the ground **shake.**
> Nobody **hears** the bell **ring.**
> They **make** the boys **clean** their room.

In each of these sentences, the first verb is finite (see A4:5 and 6) and agrees with its subject. The second verb is an infinitive. Infinitives and participles do not agree with subjects.

Some people, in using this sentence pattern, make the second verb agree with either the word coming before it, or with the subject of the sentence. This is wrong:

X *They feel the ground <u>shakes</u>*

Be on the look-out for this sentence pattern, which is:

SUBJECT - FINITE VERB - OBJECT - INFINITIVE

Remember that only the first verb, the finite verb, agrees with the subject. The second verb does not agree with anything.

Often the present tense is used in sentences such as these to dramatize past events. (see E2:1.3.)

For this sentence pattern in the past tense, see F7:3.

2. The Subjunctive

2.1 (a) We suggest that you **take** the morning flight.
We suggest that he **take** the morning flight.
We suggest that they **take** the morning flight.

(b) It is essential that you **submit** your application on time.
It is essential that the applicant **submit** her application on time.
It is essential that applicants **submit** their applications on time.

(c) People are requesting that we **extend** our opening hours.
People are requesting that the office **extend** its opening hours.
People are requesting that I **extend** my opening hours.

2.2 The verbs in bold type above are in the **subjunctive mood.** In each of these sentences somebody is being urged to do something. These same ideas could be expressed differently:

> We think you should take the morning flight.
>
> The applicant must submit her application on time.
>
> People are asking us to extend our opening hours.

The difference is that sentence patterns (a), (b) and (c) above are used in more formal speaking and writing.

2.3 In sentence patterns (a), (b) and (c), the action that is being advocated is expressed in a subordinate clause beginning with **that**. The verb in that clause is in the subjunctive mood.

2.4 For the subjunctive mood, the bare form of the verb (the infinitive without **to**) is used. It remains the same with all subjects. (It also remains the same in past tense sentences – see F7:5.)

When you use this sentence pattern, **never** add an **s** to the verb in the second clause. There is no subject-verb agreement with the subjunctive. These are incorrect:

> X We suggest that he <u>takes</u> the morning flight.
>
> X It is essential that the applicant <u>submits</u> her application on time.
>
> X People are requesting that the office <u>extends</u> its opening hours.

E18 Practice

1. Correct the wrong verb forms in these sentences:
   (a) *Unlike other politicians, Romain does not forgets the people of his constituency.*
   (b) *Why must one person holds all of us to ransom?*
   (c) *She do not returns home from work until after 11.00 p.m.*
   (d) *It may seems unbelievable, but it is true.*
   (e) *He does not has any bitterness.*

2. Change the verb in these sentences by adding the modal auxiliary given. For example:

   > You **agree** with everything he says. (must)
   > You **must agree** with everything he says.

   (a) The Parent-Teachers' Association boasts of a vibrant membership. (can)
   (b) He turns off all the lights in the building. (must)
   (c) Female members participate equally at all levels of the organization. (may)
   (d) Each student chooses a different topic. (can)
   (e) First-formers sit in the library unsupervised. (may)

3. Convert the new sentences that you have created at 2. above into the question form. For example:

   > You must agree with everything he says.
   > Must you agree with everything he says?

4. Make the new sentences that you have created at 2. above negative. For example:

   > You must agree with everything he says.
   > You must not agree with everything he says.

5. Make as many sentences as you can from this substitution table:

The principal She Mrs McGregor Father Julien	makes watches lets	the children Gavin Roach	march around the playing field. play near the office. work.
I The teachers They The visiting School Inspectors	make watch let	the class delinquent pupils the younger boys a senior student	cringe. clean the yard. laugh. cry. collect the exercise books.

6. Make as many sentences as you can from this substitution table:

I They The neighbours	hear		move. fall. stumble.
She The boy Minika	hears	someone my mother Mr James the woman	breathe. gasp. cough. cry out. slam the door. start up the car. strike a match.

7. Put suitable verbs in the blank slots. (Remember to use the infinitive form without **to**):
   (a) They see the bird _____ out the window.
   (b) Everyone feels the temperature in the room _____.
   (c) No one hears the child _____ off the bed.
   (d) I hear a clock _____ one o'clock.
   (e) The fisherman sees lightning _____ across the sky.

Present Simple Tense E18

8. Make as many sentences as you can from this substitution table:

I would like to suggest The Bureau recommends We are proposing It is imperative The writer of this article advocates Community leaders have requested We consider it essential They are insisting It is very important Circumstances require	that	employees this person householders every citizen the taxpayer you Mr Rampersad young and old alike everyone	adhere to regulations. participate in the campaign. play a more active role. join a community organization. vote in the coming elections. accept these changes. be more vigilant. file a complaint.

9. Put suitable verbs in the blank slots. Note that these clauses call for verbs in the subjunctive voice:

   (a) The doctor has recommended that Greta _____ smoking.
   (b) In this situation, it is important that we _____ loyal to each other.
   (c) The Permanent Secretary insists that you _____ your request in writing.
   (d) No one is suggesting that he _____ his responsibilities.
   (e) It is essential that the government _____ a new approach.

10. Correct the errors in the following sentences.

   (a) *It is recommended that one enrolls in a driving school.*
   (b) *It is therefore necessary that citizens are free to own firearms as a means of protecting themselves.*
   (c) *We consider it imperative that sex education focuses on abstinence.*
   (d) *Teachers are demanding that the expulsion of students is an option available to the school.*
   (e) *It is important that he studies for the examination.*

Answers pp. 261-262

E19 THE VERB *TO BE*: QUESTION FORM

1. **For questions, the verb to be simply exchanges places with its subject.** The verb goes first and the subject follows:

   STATEMENT   QUESTION
   That is a Julie mango.   **Is that** a Julie mango?
   I am late.   **Am I** late?
   You are in the right place. **Are you** in the right place?
   They are Methodists.   **Are they** Methodists?

2. **CREOLE GRAMMAR**

STATEMENT	QUESTION
Trinidadian	
I late.	I late?
You in the right place.	You in the right place?
Them is Methodist.	Them is Methodist?
Jamaican	
Me late.	Me late?
You deh in the right place.	You deh in the right place?
Them a Methodist.	Them a Methodist?

E19 Practice

1. Make as many sentences as you can from these substitution tables:

A. (a)

Am	I	
Is	he Savitri the woman Mr Darbeau this one	so insignificant? her final choice? on the list? likely to run out of gas? the last to arrive? beyond redemption? in his way?
Are	you they the Darbeaus these people Joan and Audrey	

(b) You add more items in the second and third sections of column 2. Make sure that each item agrees with the verb in column 1.

B. (a)

Why	is	that tablecloth everything our furniture the box with the books Linda's expensive briefcase	so dirty? out in the rain? a subject of controversy? on display? wet?
	are	his paintings the office files those benches my running shoes the shirts that I sent you	

(b) You add more items in each section of column 3. Make sure that each item agrees with the verb in column 2.

C. (a)

Where	is	our technician?
		the person who made the pastelles?
		Liris?
		your ID card?
		Gasparillo?
	are	all our tapes?
		the Cayman Islands?
		Mrs Quamina and her assistant?
		the results of the survey?
		Vernon's children?

(b) You add more items in each section of column 3. Make sure that each item agrees with the verb in column 2.

2. Supply suitable subjects for these sentences. Find at least five different subjects for each sentence, and say each complete sentence aloud. Use different kinds of subjects, as in **E5 Practice** 3.

   (a) Is _____ out of her mind?

   (b) Are _____ likely to accept the offer?

   (c) Is _____ ready?

   (d) Are _____ reliable witnesses?

E20 THE VERB *TO BE*: NEGATIVE FORM

1. For the negative form, simply place not after the verb to be. For speech and informal writing, however, contracted forms are used. The full form is used in speech for emphasis.

Affirmative	Negative
I am a plumber.	(a) I am not a plumber
	(b) I'm not a plumber.
Marva is upstairs.	(a) Marva is not upstairs.
	(b) Marva's not upstairs.
	(c) Marva isn't upstairs.
We are hungry.	(a) We are not hungry.
	(b) We're not hungry.
	(c) We aren't hungry.

Notice that **is not** and **are not** have two contracted forms each: you can shorten either the verb or the word **not**.

2. **CREOLE GRAMMAR**

> We have already seen (E5) that Creole does not make much use of the present tense form of **to be**.
> Here are the negative sentences above translated into Creole:
>
> *Trinidadian*
> I eh no plumber.
> Marva eh upstairs.
> We eh hungry.
>
> *Jamaican*
> Me no no plumber.
> Marva no deh upstairs.
> We no hungry.
> Note the double negative in the first sentence – this is not allowed in English.

3. **AVOID THESE ERRORS**

3.1 *Spelling*

Do not write

X *isnot*   X *arenot*

When the full form of the negative is used, these words are written separately:

    is not   are not

They are only joined in writing when the **not** is shortened:

    isn't   aren't

3.2 *Punctuation*

When you use the contracted forms, be sure to put in the apostrophe, and be sure to put it in the right place. Remember the apostrophe marks where a letter or letters are missing:

    I a̸m not   =   I'm not

    Carol i̸s not   =   Carol's not
    Carol is no̸t   =   Carol isn't

    You a̸re not   =   You're not
    You are no̸t   =   You aren't

3.3 *Double negatives*

Review E16. With the negative form of all verbs, watch out for the double negative:

    X *I am <u>not no</u> plumber.*
    X *You are <u>not no</u> Methodist.*

The correct forms would be:

    I am not a plumber.
    You are not a Methodist.

Or, for emphasis, one could use either **not any** or **no**:

    I am not any plumber.
    You are not any Methodist.

    I am no plumber.
    You are no Methodist.

E20 Practice

1. Make as many sentences as you can from this substitution table.

I	am not	
He Savitri The woman Mr Darbeau This one	is not isn't	so insignificant. her final choice. on the list. likely to run out of gas.
You They The Darbeaus These people Joan and Audrey	are not aren't	the last to arrive. beyond redemption. in his way.

2. Complete these sentences with the negative form of the verb **to be**, present tense. Give both full and contracted forms. For example:

   Cricket_____ my favourite sport.
   Cricket is not my favourite sport.
   Cricket isn't my favourite sport.

   (a) This _____ an open-and-shut case.
   (b) Too many people _____ aware of their rights.
   (c) It is clear that the captain _____ in charge of his crew.
   (d) You _____ as safe here as you think.
   (e) We notice that privatization and retrenchment _____ among the topics down for discussion.

3. These sentences contain double negatives. Correct each, using, where possible, the different forms shown in E20:3.3.

   (a) *The boy is not no bandit.*
   (b) *I am not nobody's slave.*
   (c) *That isn't no way to treat your child.*
   (d) *You aren't no angel yourself.*
   (e) *These young thugs are not afraid of nothing.*

   Answers p. 262

E21 THE VERB *TO BE*: NEGATIVE QUESTIONS

1. Review E17.

Formal	*Informal*
Am I not the winner?	Aren't I the winner?
Is he not on the bus?	Isn't he on the bus?
Are they not Methodists?	Aren't they Methodists?

Notice that the contracted form of **am I not** is **aren't I. Am** becomes **are**.

2. **CREOLE GRAMMAR**

Trinidadian		
I eh the winner?		Ain't I is the winner?
He eh on the bus?	OR	Ain't he on the bus?
Them eh Methodist?		Ain't them is Methodist?
Jamaican		
No me a the winner?		Don't me a the winner?
Him no deh pon the bus?	OR	Don't him deh pon the bus?
Them no Methodist?		Don't them a Methodist?

E21 Practice

1. (a) Make sentences from these substitution tables.
   (b) Add more items in each section of column 2. Make sure that each item agrees with the verb in column 1.

A.

Isn't	Christine	a little tipsy?
	your brother-in-law	ready to proceed?
	the chairperson	from St Croix?
	that juror	
	anybody here	
Aren't	Christine and her boyfriend	in the National Party?
	the workshop participants	Jamaican?
	those attendants	
	Mr Harrigin's lawyers	

B.

Is	Christine / your brother-in-law / the chairperson / that juror / anybody here	not	a little tipsy? / ready to proceed? / from St Croix? / in the National Party? / Jamaican?
Are	Christine and her boyfriend / your relatives / the workshop participants / those attendants / Mr Harrigin's lawyers		

2. Convert these sentences into negative questions. Give both full and contracted forms:

A. (a) Access to information is a basic human right.
   (b) We are under a state of emergency.
   (c) I am eligible to vote.
   (d) That is the whole point of the exercise.
   (e) Toy guns are on the Negative List.

B. (a) The County of St David is under your jurisdiction.
   (b) Rape and murder are serious crimes.
   (c) You are Miss Adeline's grandchild.
   (d) Gregory is a member of the Drama Society.
   (e) Divestment is pretty much the same as privatization.

C. (a) These people are willing to come forward.
   (b) This is a dangerous precedent.
   (c) They are on the school board.
   (d) Embezzlement is punishable by law.
   (e) Elections are due in December.

Answers pp. 262-263

F. The Past Simple Tense

F1 FORMING THE PAST SIMPLE TENSE

1. (a) The instructor **showed** us what to do.
   (b) They **changed** their clothes.
   (c) Gwendolyn **took** the child.

   The words in bold type are verbs in the past simple tense. Each refers to an action that was completed before the sentence was spoken.

   How do you form the past simple tense?

2. Regular verbs

For most verbs the past tense is formed by adding **ed** to the basic form (the infinitive):

show + **ed** = showed

If the verb already ends with an **e**, one simply adds a **d**:

change + **d** = changed.

3. Irregular verbs

Some verbs do not form their past tense in the "regular" way.

3.1 There are many important, everyday verbs which do not take on any ending. These verbs change *internally* for the past tense:

take	took
get	got
fight	fought

Two commonly-used verbs change into a completely new word for the past tense:

| go | went |
| is/are | was/were |

3.2 For some verbs that end with **d** in their bare form, **d** changes into **t**:

bend	bent
build	built
lend	lent
send	sent

3.3 Some verbs change internally *and* add a **t**:

creep	crept
feel	felt
kneel	knelt
leave	left
lose	lost

3.4 With some verbs, you can put on either **t** or **ed** for the past tense. Both are correct:

burn	burnt/burned
dream	dreamt/dreamed
lean	leant/leaned
leap	leapt/leaped
learn	learnt/learned
smell	smelt/smelled
spell	spelt/spelled
spill	spilt/spilled

(You will find full lists of irregular verbs in almost all English grammar books.)

4. NB: Note on spelling

For verbs ending in **y**, the rules for adding **ed** are the same as for adding **s** to words ending in **y**. See C2:4.

– If there is a vowel before the **y**, simply add **ed**:

   stay - stayed   prey - preyed   destroy - destroyed

– If there is a consonant before the **y,** you must first change the **y** into **i** before adding **ed**:

   cry - cried   identify - identified   tidy - tidied

However, there are some important exceptions to these rules, for example:

   pay - paid   say - said   lay - laid

   fly - flew

5. **CREOLE GRAMMAR**

> Gwendolyn **take** the child.
>
> Them **change** fe them clothes.
>
> These sentences express completed action. You will notice that the bare form of the verb is used for this purpose.
>
> In Creole some speaking situations call for the use of **did** before the verb to show past tense (see G3:3 and G4:5.3):
>
> Gwendolyn **did take** the child.
>
> Them **did change** fe them clothes.
>
> In either case the main verb is in its bare form. To show completed action in Creole we either use the bare form of the verb on its own, or the bare form with a separate past tense marker.

Creole speakers when using English often neglect to change the form of the verb into the English past tense, because the bare form of the verb gives the Creole speaker the "feel" of completed action.

F1 Practice

1. Identify verbs in the past simple tense in the following sentences.

A. (a) The organizers cleaned the place afterwards.

  (b) They appeared in court on Wednesday.

  (c) Trevor and Naima entered the race this year.

  (d) Today work stopped on that project.

  (e) One group worked upstairs and another downstairs.

B. (a) They became very fit.

  (b) The driver found my briefcase on the bus.

  (c) Finally they began to see signs of progress.

  (d) The school gave him another chance.

  (e) The photographer took a picture of that for the records.

C. (a) After the last party they left the place in a mess.

  (b) Sylvie crept nervously out of the house.

  (c) The graduating class bought a farewell present for their teacher.

  (d) Sylvie felt weak.

  (e) At the beginning of the school year they spent a fortune on books and uniforms.

Past Simple Tense F1

2. Begin each of the following sentences with the phrase given, changing the verb to the past simple tense, for example:

> In 1980...
> Social workers visit the home on a regular basis.
>
> In 1980 social workers visited the home on a regular basis.

If you are unsure of the past tense form of any verb, consult a dictionary.

A. In 1980...
   (a) These two farms supply vegetables for the School Feeding Programme.
   (b) Government ministries owe large sums of money to the Water and Sewerage Authority.
   (c) Rank-and-file members of the party support this decision.
   (d) That sugar estate pays its workers a bonus.
   (e) Notices go out by mail to all of the branches.

B. During that period...
   (a) Mr Barnes controls everything.
   (b) Public health care facilities stay open on weekends.
   (c) The animals sleep under the house.
   (d) Michael and his sister sing in the church choir.
   (e) Farmers build makeshift stalls along the roadside to sell their produce.

C. A few months ago...
   (a) The school looks almost new.
   (b) Teachers call that boy brilliant.
   (c) Ms Ramdeen chairs the general meeting.
   (d) We are under a state of emergency.
   (e) The people of this community know very little about drugs.

Answers p. 263

F2 VERBS WHICH DO NOT CHANGE

1. There are some verbs which in English do not change their form for the past tense:

    We **shut** all the windows last night.
    The electricity pole fell when the truck **hit** it.

2. **The verb read is written the same for the past and present tense, but is pronounced differently. In the past tense it is pronounced "red".**

3. Here is a list of verbs which remain the same in the past tense:

beat	cast	hit	set
bet	cost	hurt	shut
broadcast	cut	let	split
burst	forecast	put	spread

4. **The verb to cost has two different meanings, and for each the past tense is different.**

    4.1 (a) This schoolbook **costs** $195.00 [Present]

    (b) A few years ago this schoolbook **cost** $30.00. [Past]

    In these sentences **to cost** means "to carry a price". The past tense of this verb is **cost**.

    4.2 (a) The builder **costs** all the materials and gives you an estimate for the repairs. [Present]

    (b) The builder **costed** all the materials and gave us an estimate for the repairs. [Past]

    In these sentences (4.2 (a) and (b), **to cost** means "to find out, or to calculate the cost of". The past tense of the verb, when it is used in this sense, is **costed**.

F2 Practice

1. Identify verbs in the past simple tense in the following sentences:

    (a) A police officer read Craig the warrant on the spot.

    (b) First they cut down the thick bush.

    (c) St Mary's beat us in the first game.

    (d) A few years ago a loaf of bread like that cost only ten cents.

    (e) In the 1980s this station broadcast to the whole region

2. Begin each of the following sentences with the phrase given, changing the verbs to the past simple tense. (See F1-Practice 2.) In each sentence there is more than one verb to be changed.

On that day...

(a) The pressure increases to the point where some water mains burst, so that repair crews have to work overtime.
(b) When she gets home from work, she shuts the gate and lets the dog out of its kennel.
(c) Rumours spread like wildfire and immediately people begin to congregate in the main square.
(d) Getting to the airport costs me $75 because I have to take a taxi.
(e) The ringleader keeps the lion's share of the money, and members of the gang split the rest among themselves.

Answers p. 264

F3 PAST TENSE VERBS IN JOINED SENTENCES

Remember that many sentences are really two or more sentences or clauses joined together. Therefore many sentences contain more than one verb to be given the correct form. Often we give one verb the correct form and miss, or ignore, any others:

X *Kenwyn ran down the hill and <u>call</u> his friends.*
X *Before he left the house he <u>clean</u> and <u>scrub</u> every room.*

The correct forms are:

Kenwyn ran down the hill and called his friends.
Before he left the house he cleaned and scrubbed every room.

Be sure to recognize all the past tense verbs in the sentence and give them their past tense form. (Compare E7.)

F3 Practice

1. In each of the following sentences, replace the verb in bold type with each of the verbs given, in the past simple tense:

Say the new sentences aloud before writing them down.

The Knots In English

A. Mr Dennis went to the nearest hardware store and **bought** a wrench.
   (a) to steal
   (b) to borrow
   (c) to pick up
   (d) to get
   (e) to select

B. When I contacted the officer, he **informed** me that the complaint was under investigation.
   (a) to assure
   (b) to tell
   (c) to notify
   (d) to remind
   (e) to advise

C. The Principal called the three students into her office and **scolded** them for what they had done.
   (a) to reprimand
   (b) to praise
   (c) to upbraid
   (d) to commend
   (e) to reward

D. A group of irate farmers came into town on a truck and **dumped** their rotten produce on the steps of the Hall of Justice.
   (a) to offload
   (b) to deposit
   (c) to leave
   (d) to throw
   (e) to spread

E. Everybody rose with one accord and **cheered** noisily until the meeting was called to order.
   (a) to clap
   (b) to protest
   (c) to argue
   (d) to applaud
   (e) to chant

2. Correct the wrong verbs in the following sentences.

   (a) *Many families left their homes and travel far in search of a better life.*

   (b) *The government demolished the old courthouse and build a new one on the same spot.*

   (c) *Some schoolchildren went and raid Mr Henry's mango tree.*

   (d) *I started out quite well, but as time goes by it became more difficult for me.*

   (e) *The telephone company came yesterday and fix the phone as soon as I call them.*

   Answers p. 264

F4 VERBS ENDING WITH A SOUND LIKE D

Often when the verb is a word which ends with **d** or **t**, people think of that sound as a past tense ending, and they use the word as it is for the past tense:

   X *The PTA <u>hold</u> an emergency meeting to discuss the teachers' strike.*
   X *Many people in this constituency <u>support</u> you in the last election.*

Be on the look-out for verbs like these. The **d** or **t** is *part of the word*, so for the past tense you still have to make a change:

   The PTA **held** an emergency meeting....
   Many people in this constituency **supported** you....

   (Compare E12.)

F4 Practice

1. Begin each of the following sentences with the phrase given, changing the verb to the past simple tense. (See **F1 Practice** 2.)

A. At first...

   (a) Participants adopt a cautious attitude.

   (b) I need proof of their good intentions.

   (c) The older people reject these sudden changes.

   (d) Exhibitions like these attract only a small crowd.

   (e) His former classmates avoid him like the plague.

B. In July of that year...

   (a) Their confrontations result in violence.

   (b) Still too many obstacles stand in the way.

(c) They disconnect the electricity supply for nonpayment of arrears.

(d) The authorities limit the movements of foreigners.

(e) Talks between the two parties inevitably end on a sour note.

2. Correct the wrong verbs in the following sentences:

   (a) *I attend St Mary's Primary School for three years, but later moved to another school.*

   (b) *My aunt was not a rich person, but she assist us when we couldn't make ends meet.*

   (c) *Before that centre was opened, many AIDS victims end their days on the pavements of the city because their families refused to have anything to do with them.*

   (d) *When the accountant add the figures, she realized that there was a shortfall.*

   (e) *The French and the British fight over this island throughout the eighteenth century.*

   Answers p. 264

F5 QUESTION FORM OF THE PAST SIMPLE TENSE

1. Review E14:3. For the question form of the past tense, the same process takes place as for the present tense, except that the auxiliary **to do** is in the past tense: **did**.

Statement	Question
This team **won** the match.	**Did** this team **win** the match?
She **planted** the mango tree.	**Did** she **plant** the mango tree?

2. **CREOLE GRAMMAR**

Statement	Question
This team win the match.	This team win the match?
She plant the mango tree.	She plant the mango tree?
This team did win the match.	This team did win the match?
She did plant the mango tree.	She did plant the mango tree?
In Creole, the question form is the same as the statement form. (See E14.)	

3. Remember that in English the following would not be real questions (see E14:2):

   You wanted a ticket?
   The uncle came to the wedding?

   The English question form needs to be practised.

F5 Practice

1. Make sentences from these substitution tables.

A.

Did	anybody	take notes?
	the caretaker of the property	object to being disturbed?
	your mother	give you permission?
	the police officers on duty	demand money?
	Mr Ramkissoon's secretary	respond to their request?
	Ms Sutherland	commit the alleged offences?
	Cecil or any of his assistants	know that this would happen?

B.

Why	did	all those people	agree to such a thing?
When		you	get involved in the scheme?
How		the other lady	make that large downpayment?
		shareholders	contact the police?
		your client	begin to suspect that something was wrong?

2. Convert the following statements into questions:

A. (a) Allyson got the contract.
   (b) The organizers cleaned the place afterwards.
   (c) Trevor and Naima entered the race this year.
   (d) The school gave him another chance.
   (e) They appeared in court on Wednesday.

B. (a) He told them to go down Grant Street.
   (b) They went straight down the road.
   (c) Ma Charlotte walked to the market last Saturday.
   (d) The children found that film boring.
   (e) He put a boiled egg in his lunch kit.

Answers p. 264

F6 NEGATIVE FORM OF THE PAST SIMPLE TENSE

1. Review E15:1. The structure is the same for the past tense, with did as the auxiliary.

Affirmative

Gwendolyn **took** the child.

They **changed** their clothes.

Negative

Gwendolyn **did not take** the child.
Gwendolyn **didn't take** the child.

They **did not change** their clothes.
They **didn't change** their clothes.

2. **CREOLE GRAMMAR**

> In Trinidadian Creole one makes past tense verbs negative by placing either **didn't** or **eh** before them. The two forms are subtly different in meaning.
>
> > Gwendolyn didn't take the child.
> > They didn't change they clothes.
>
> With **eh** the meaning is closer to the English present perfect tense (see G3:3):
>
> > Gwendolyn eh take the child.
> > They eh change they clothes.
>
> When **eh** is used with a verb of mental action, that verb is in the present tense (see E15:3):
>
> > Craig **eh care** if Good Friday fall on Ash Wednesday.
>
> In Jamaican Creole, either **no** or **never** is placed before the verb to make it negative:
>
> > Gwendolyn no take the pickney.
> > Them no change fe them clothes.
>
> > Gwendolyn never take the pickney.
> > Them never change fe them clothes.

3. **AVOID THESE ERRORS**

   3.1 *Double negatives*

   Review E16. Everything in E16 applies also to the past tense. These sentences are incorrect in English:

   X *I didn't want none.*
   X *The children didn't know nothing.*
   X *They didn't get no back pay.*

Past Simple Tense **F6**

In English the correct forms are:

> I didn't want any.
> The children didn't know anything.
> They didn't get any back pay.

3.2 *Spelling*

When you use the full form of the negative, do not join the auxiliary to **not**. This is incorrect:

> X *didnot*

These words must always be written separately:

> did not

It is only when **not** is contracted, or shortened, that it is joined to **did**:

> didn't

3.3 *Punctuation*

When you use the contracted form, do not forget the apostrophe, and do not put it in the wrong place.

These are incorrect:

> X *did'nt*   X *didnt'*

The apostrophe is used to show where a letter is missing. The missing letter is the **o** in **not**, so the apostrophe belongs in the space between **n** and **t**:

> didn't

F6 Practice

1. Make the following sentences negative by changing the verb, using the full and contracted forms. For example:

    Social workers visited the home on a regular basis.

    Social workers did not visit the home on a regular basis.

    Social workers didn't visit the home on a regular basis.

The Knots In English

A. (a) Allyson got the contract.
   (b) The organizers cleaned the place afterwards.
   (c) Trevor and Naima entered the race this year.
   (d) The school gave him another chance.
   (e) They appeared in court on Wednesday.

B. (a) He told them to go down Grant Street.
   (b) They went straight down the road.
   (c) Ma Charlotte walked to the market last Saturday.
   (d) The children found that film boring.
   (e) He put an egg in his lunch kit.

2. Correct the errors in the following sentences.
   (a) *I told you that I didn't see no man working in the garden.*
   (b) *That generation of people didnot have such wide choices.*
   (c) *At the time it did'nt seem to be such a bad idea.*
   (d) *We went from store to store looking for black sequins but we didn't find none.*
   (e) *The child didn't eat nothing before he left home.*

   Answers p. 265

F7 WHEN NOT TO USE PAST TENSE FORM

1. The infinitive

Some people change every verb in sight into the past tense, just to be on the safe side. However, it is wrong to change verbs that are in the **infinitive** form to the past tense. (See A4:3.1.)

The following are situations in which the infinitive is used, and where the error is often made of turning it into the past tense.

2. Infinitive with auxiliary

2.1 The error frequently occurs with the use of the question and negative forms of past tense verbs. In these forms the verb has two parts: **did** + infinitive. (See F5 and F6.) Sentences such as these are often produced:

> X Why did you <u>wrote</u> that insulting letter?
> X The speaker did not <u>minced</u> words.

The correct forms are:

> Why **did** you **write** that insulting letter?
> The speaker **did** not **mince** words.

2.2 Here it is the auxiliary that indicates the tense of the whole verb. The auxiliary **to do** is in the past tense: **did**; therefore the verb is marked past tense. The other part of the verb is never marked for tense.

2.3 Some people convert the infinitive part of the verb into a past tense form even when the verb is not past tense:

> X Does the floating of the TT dollar <u>caused</u> more harm than good?
> X One may <u>asked</u> who is responsible.
> X You must <u>used</u> a thicker brush.

These should be:

> **Does** the floating of the TT dollar **cause** more harm than good?
> One **may ask** who is responsible.
> You **must use** a thicker brush.

2.4 There are certain auxiliaries which are always followed by the infinitive, and when we form verbs with these auxiliaries we must remember to leave the infinitive alone:

(a) do/does/did

(b) can/could

(c) may/might

(d) shall/should

(e) will/would

(f) must

2.5 One of the reasons why people make the error we are discussing here is that there are forms of the verb in English which **seem** to be made up of an auxiliary and a "past tense" form.

These are the perfect tenses and the passive voice (see G3, G4 and G5). In these verb forms, however, the second part of the verb is the past **participle,** not past tense, and the auxiliaries are **to have** and **to be**, never the ones given at (a)–(f) above:

> The floating of the TT dollar **has caused** more harm than good.
> For this kind of work a thicker brush **is used.**

3. Infinitive with another verb

See E18:1.3. In this sentence pattern, even when the first verb is in the past tense, the second one remains unchanged because it is an infinitive:

> I **watched** the bottle **fall** to the floor.
> Somebody **saw** her **take** the money.
> He **felt** the ground **shake**.
> Nobody **heard** the bell **ring**.
> They **made** the boys **clean** their room.
> Sylvia **let** the animals **run** free.

Sometimes **to have** is used in this way with a second verb:

> The scoutmaster **had** us **dig** a trench around the campsite.

Do not be tempted to make the second verb past tense. These sentences are incorrect:

> X He felt the ground <u>shook</u>.
> X They made the boys <u>cleaned</u> their room.

4. Infinitive with "to"

It might be difficult to recognize the infinitive when it occurs without **to** in front of it. But when a verb is preceded by **to** it is clearly the infinitive and must never be made past tense. This is, however, a common error:

> X Different methods should be used to <u>convinced</u> the public.
> X To <u>missed</u> that opportunity would be a mistake.
> X They decided not to <u>pursued</u> the matter.

The correct forms are:

> Different methods should be used to convince the public.
> To miss that opportunity would be a mistake.
> They decided not to pursue the matter.

5. The subjunctive

Review E18:2.

Here is this same type of sentence in the past tense:

> (a) We **suggested** that they **take** the morning flight.
> (b) It **was** essential that you **submit** your application on time.
> (c) People **were requesting** that we **extend** our opening hours.

Note that the second verb in each sentence is **not** in the past tense form. That verb is in the subjunctive mood, for which the bare form (the infinitive, without **to**) is used.

This would be wrong:

X *We suggested that they <u>took</u> the morning flight.*

F7 Practice

1. Make sentences from this substitution table.

Somebody	saw	Gary	fall.
We	heard	the older girl	climb the stairs.
Mr Narine	made	some workmen	ring the bell.
The neighbours	watched	Ema	turn on the generator.
Leader Paul	let	the children	start the car.
			close the door.

2. Put suitable verbs in the blank slots. (Remember to use the infinitive form without **to**.):
   (a) They saw the bird _____ out the window.
   (b) Everyone felt the temperature in the room _____.
   (c) No one heard the child _____ off the bed.
   (d) I heard a clock _____ one o'clock.
   (e) The fisherman saw lightning _____ across the sky.

3. Make sentences from this substitution table:

The Commission of Enquiry	requested		students observe the dress code.
Several prominent persons	recommended		the company recall this product.
Organizations across the country	advocated		the Licensing Authority impose harsher fines.
A previous administration	proposed		
	suggested	that	
	saw it as mandatory		corporal punishment be only a last resort.
	considered it imperative		Parliament amend the Constitution.

4. Put suitable verbs in the blank slots. Note that these clauses call for verbs in the subjunctive mood:

   (a) Some people were suggesting that the government _____ the curfew.
   (b) One of the recommendations put forward was that children under twelve _____ free of charge.
   (c) The National Cultural Council proposed that the country's leading theatre groups _____ a conference.
   (d) My uncle wrote a letter requesting that the family _____ him legal custody of the boy.
   (e) The School Board made it mandatory that parents or guardians _____ the school at least once every term.

5. Correct the errors in the following sentences:

A. (a) *I forgot to signed the form.*
   (b) *He saw the man struck his wife with a hoe.*
   (c) *In what year did this country changed over to the metric system?*
   (d) *During the cholera alert, the Ministry of Health recommended that we boiled all drinking water.*
   (e) *Judging by the performances of the present day athletes one may agreed with this, but we must take a closer look to make a fair comparison.*

B. (a) *Did they conduct surveys or assessed the environmental impact?*
   (b) *News of the gas leak was suppressed because the authorities did not want to alarmed the population.*
   (c) *What makes me admired this man most is his honesty.*
   (d) *Yesterday I heard a certain caller from Tunapuna quoted the National Anthem.*
   (e) *The manager did not said anything about overtime.*

Answers p. 265

F8 THE VERB *TO BE*: PAST SIMPLE TENSE

1. To be is the only verb which requires subject-verb agreement in the past tense.

SUBJECT	VERB
I/he/she/it Nesta/the dog	was
you/we/they people/the dogs Carol and Earl	were

Review E5:1. In the past simple tense, the verb **to be** has only two forms (and not three as in the present simple tense).

All singular subjects take **was**. The exception is **you**, which, for subject-verb agreement, is always treated as plural.

2. **It might be useful to know, however, that you really is plural.** The English language once had a singular and plural form for this pronoun. These are the forms that we meet in old texts such as the Bible.

The singular form was **thou** for the subject of a sentence and **thee** in the object slot. The plural was **ye** for subjects and **you** in the object slot.

Thou, thee and **ye** have been lost, and in modern English the plural form **you** serves as both singular and plural (as well as subject and object).

Creole, like many other languages, has singular and plural forms for this pronoun: **yu** and **allyu** in Trinidadian Creole, and **yu** and **oono** in Jamaican.

3. **Question form**

Subject and verb are inverted for the question form as in the present tense of the verb **to be** (see E19). Verb goes before subject:

Statement:	**Corporal Henry was** in the station. **The oranges were** ripe.
Question:	**Was Corporal Henry** in the station? **Were the oranges** ripe?

4. Negative

For the negative form the verb is followed by **not** which is contracted in speech and informal writing. The full form may be used in speech for emphasis:

>Corporal Henry was not in the station.
>Corporal Henry wasn't in the station.
>
>The oranges were not ripe.
>The oranges weren't ripe.

Note carefully the spelling and punctuation of full and contracted forms.
Beware of double negatives. (See E20:3.)

5. Negative questions

See E17 and E21.

>Wasn't Corporal Henry in the station?
>Was Corporal Henry not in the station?
>
>Weren't the oranges ripe?
>Were the oranges not ripe?

Be sure to put the apostrophe in the correct place.

6. Special note on "I"

6.1 When it comes to subject-verb agreement, most singular subjects can be relied upon to follow a set rule. Most singular subjects take the **s** form of the verb:

>The driver **talks**
>Gary **has**
>A boat **is**
>She **was**

6.2 We have already seen (F8:2) that **you** is really plural, which is why it does whatever other plural subjects do. Plural subjects, including **you,** take the form of the verb with no **s** ending:

The drivers **talk**	You **talk**
Gary and Freda **have**	You **have**
Boats **are**	You **are**
They **were**	You **were**

6.3 The first person singular pronoun **I**, however, does not stay with any one group of subjects for all verbs:

(a) With the present simple tense of ordinary verbs, it behaves like a plural subject:

>I **talk**
>I **have**

(b) With the present tense of the verb **to be** it stands apart from all other subjects and has its own verb:

>I **am**

(c) With the past tense of the verb **to** be it rejoins other singular subjects:

>I **was**
>The driver **was**
>Freda **was**

7. **CREOLE GRAMMAR**

>In basic Creole the verb **did** is an alternative to **was**:
>>It did late already.
>>It was late already.
>
>Creole uses **was** with all subjects:
>>You was we friend.
>>She was we friend.
>>Them was we friend.
>
>Therefore when using **to be** in English, both past and present, it is important that we remember to use the form that agrees with the subject.

8. **In using was and were, you also need to remember all the many pitfalls of subject-verb agreement shown in E6-E13.**

F8 Practice

1. Make sentences from this substitution table.

I The girl at the desk Machel Everybody here She He	was	at the funeral. glad to go home. out for the day. ready to start a fight. on the TV news. downstairs. too busy to notice.
Joy and Doolarie All her sons These vendors You They The older tenants	were	

2. Put the correct form, **was** or **were,** into the blank slots:
    (a) My great-aunt, who lived to the age of one hundred and four, _____ a vegetarian.
    (b) The receptionist told me that you _____ the person to see.
    (c) I took one look at them and realized that they _____ plainclothes police officers.
    (d) The salary they offered him _____ an insult.
    (e) Immigration authorities refused to let them in because they _____ Rastafarians.

3. Convert these statements into questions, beginning each with the word given, for example:
    Why...
    Vernon was late for the performance.
    Why was Vernon late for the performance?

A. Why...
    (a) The two boys were still outside at 9.00 o'clock.
    (b) You were such a coward.
    (c) Miriam's watch was in the fridge.

(d) Certain people were reluctant to come forward.

  (e) Nobody was there to receive us.

B. When...

  (a) Roanna was in the bank.

  (b) Maurice Bishop was Prime Minister of Grenada.

  (c) You were a fashion model.

  (d) This gentleman was on the Board of Trustees.

  (e) Government ministers were accountable to the people.

4. Complete these sentences with the negative form of the verb **to be**, past simple tense. Give both full and contracted forms. For example:

   > Cricket _____ my favourite sport.
   > Cricket was not my favourite sport.
   > Cricket wasn't my favourite sport.

   (a) Breaking the news _____ a pleasant task.

   (b) Those two names _____ on the passenger list.

   (c) You _____ the only latecomer.

   (d) The security guard _____ there at the time.

   (e) Our friends _____ too keen on the new arrangements

5. Turn the following statements into negative questions. Use the contracted form. For example:

   > Vernon was late for the performance.
   > Wasn't Vernon late for the performance?

   (a) Miriam's watch was in the fridge.

   (b) Certain people were reluctant to come forward.

   (c) You were a fashion model.

   (d) This gentleman was on the Board of Trustees.

   (e) Government Ministers were accountable to the people.

6. In some of the following sentences the verb **to be** does not agree with its subject. Correct this error where it occurs.

   (a) *Our flight landed in Barbados on time, but then there were a long delay.*

(b) *One of the women was pregnant.*

(c) *Most of the people killed in the uprising was Muslims.*

(d) *One of the more strict school rules were that smoking was prohibited on the school compound.*

(e) *Relations between Wesley and his father were less than cordial.*

Answers pp. 265-266

F9 *WERE* IN IF-CLAUSES

1. Look at these sentence patterns:

    (a) **If I were** in a better financial position, I would help you.

    (b) He spends money **as if it were** something that grew on trees.

    (c) They behaved **as though the danger were** past.

    (d) **If the price of oil were** to fall any lower, our economy would collapse.

    (e) I wish **he were** better equipped to deal with this situation.

    (f) **Were I** your mother, you would not be wearing such clothes.

    In each of these sentences, there is a clause expressing something that is not real but imagined. It is the clause in which **were** is used.

    Were here does not indicate past tense.
    Were in these clauses indicates unreality. We can call these "if-clauses".
    Used in this way, **were** is a subjunctive form.

2. **Notice that there is no subject-verb agreement. In if-clauses, were is used with all subjects.**

    However, in informal English **was** may be used in this kind of clause. (That is, of course, if the subject agrees with **was**.) The exception is sentence pattern (f). You cannot say:

    X <u>Was</u> I your mother, you...

F9 Practice

Make sentences from these substitution tables.

A.

You speak as though I wish that What if Stop acting as though	he were already on the land. Sybil were here with us. my family were rich. the deadline were months away. you were ten years younger. this whole thing were an illusion. there were some viable alternative.

B.

If this were another country If it were to rain tomorrow If they were in charge If he were to give the order If something like that were to happen If this news were to spread If people were really up in arms	the match would be postponed. everything would come to a standstill. the day would be declared a public holiday. the relevant departments would have to take swift action. there would be serious repercussions.

F10 *COULD* AND *WOULD*

Could and **would** are modal auxiliaries (see E18:1.2) used for a number of different purposes.

1. Past simple tense

In Standard English **could** and **would** are the past tense forms of **can** and **will**:

Present	Past
can	could
will	would

1.1 CREOLE GRAMMAR

> 1.1.1 The Trinidadian type of Creole uses **could** as the present tense of **to be able**, i.e., Trinidadian Creole uses **could** where Standard English uses **can**:
>
> He have good lyrics, but you could sing better than he.
>
> The negative, however, is **can't** (pronounced **car**, or **cyar**, or **cyan**):
>
> You can't put that there.
>
> 1.1.2 One of the ways of forming the future tense in Trinidadian Creole is to place **would** before the verb, where Standard English uses **will**:
>
> I would give you the answer next week.
>
> If you don't behave, you wouldn't get nothing for Christmas.
>
> (The Creole future tense is also formed by placing one of the following before the verb: **go, going, going to, going and**.)

1.2 In Standard English the present tense form of **to be able** is **can**; and **will** is the auxiliary used to form the future tense of verbs.

The following are therefore incorrect English sentences:

X (a) *This elevator <u>could</u> only accommodate ten people, so two of you have to get out.*

X (b) *The Minister of Finance <u>would</u> present the Budget in Parliament at 2.00 o'clock this afternoon.*

The correct forms are:

(a) This elevator can only accommodate ten people, so two of you have to get out.

(b) The Minister of Finance will present the Budget in Parliament at 2.00 o'clock this afternoon.

In (a) the speaker is talking about a situation which exists *now*, that is to say while he/she is speaking.

The verb must therefore be in the present tense: **can**.

It would only be appropriate to use **could** if the speaker were giving an account of something that happened **before the time of speaking**, i.e., past tense:

The elevator could only accommodate ten people, so two of them had to get out.

In (b) the speaker is referring to something that is going to happen. It hasn't happened yet. It is still in the future.

For this in English one has to use **will**, not **would.**

> **Will** means "is going to".
>
> **Would** means "was going to". (Its other meanings are discussed in 2. – 4. below.)

If you use **would** it means that the event is not ahead of you – *not* in the future. It means that the event is actually behind you:

> When the news got around that the Minister of Finance would present the Budget in Parliament at 2.00 o'clock that afternoon, a feeling of mild dread came over the population.

1.3 Not only do some people use **could** and **would** in English sentences which call for **can** and **will**. Some of us make the opposite error: using **can** and **will** where English requires **could** and **would**.

In English **can** and **will** are not normally used in past tense contexts. These sentences are incorrect:

> X *I didn't believe that I <u>can</u> finish in time.*
> X *They followed him to see which road he <u>will</u> take.*

In past tense sentences you must use **could** and **would**:

> I didn't believe that I could finish in time.
> They followed him to see which road he would take.

1.4 The question and negative forms (with contractions) are:

Question

| Can/will he take...? | Could/would he take...? |

Negative

| He cannot/will not take... | He could not/would not take... |
| He can't/won't take... | He couldn't/wouldn't take... |

Negative questions

| Can he not/will he not take...? | Could he not/would he not take...? |
| Can't he/won't he take? | Couldn't he/wouldn't he take...? |

NB: The past tense of the modal **may** is **might**.
The past tense of the modal **must** is **must** – no change.

STOP HERE AND DO F10 PRACTICE 1. – 3.

2. Conditional sentences

2.1 We have already seen (F9) how the past tense form of a verb may be used to express not past time but unreality. **Could** and **would** are used for this purpose in sentences which carry a condition (an if-clause, stated or not), if that condition is unreal or unlikely. These are known as conditional sentences:

(a) She **could destroy** his reputation if she **chose** to.

(b) Your father **could lend** you a few dollars.

(c) Nobody **would object** to a rise in salary if the company **were to offer** one.

(d) A wrench **would solve** the problem.

In (a) and (c) there is an if-clause attached. There is no stated if-clause in (b) and (d), but an if-clause (or condition) is implied. (Make up likely if-clauses for (b) and (d).)

Sometimes the if-clause begins with **unless**, which means "if not":

(e) Nobody would object to a rise in salary, unless he were a millionaire.

2.2 The sentences (a) to (e) above refer to the present time, even though their verbs are in the past tense form. Conditional sentences are also made with present tense verbs, but their meaning is different:

> She **can destroy** his reputation if she **chooses** to.
> Nobody **will object** to a rise in salary if the company **offers** one.

In these sentences the condition (expressed in the if-clause) is not definitely untrue or unlikely. This speaker sees the condition as something that may or may not happen.

In sentences (a) and (c) above, where the verbs in the if-clause are in the past tense form, the speaker is expressing some doubt as to whether the condition will become a reality.

2.3 If conditional sentences referring to the present use past tense verbs, what tenses are used in conditional sentences referring to the past?

In the if-clause you use the past perfect (see G4), and in the main clause you use **could have** or **would have** followed by a past participle (see G1):

(e) She **could have destroyed** his reputation if she **had chosen** to.

(f) Your father **could have lent** you a few dollars.

(g) Nobody **would have objected** to a rise in salary if the company **had offerred** one.

(h) A wrench **would have solved** the problem.

In all of these sentences, the verbs refer to actions which **might have** but **did not** happen – possibilities that did not materialize.

2.4 **Could have** is also used to mean not that the thing did not happen, but that the speaker is only speculating:

> It **could have been** an electrical fault that caused the fire.

2.5 **CREOLE GRAMMAR**

> 2.5.1 In Creole **could have** and **would have** (pronounced "coulda" and "woulda") are also used in conditional sentences referring to the past, i.e., to speak of things which did not actually happen:
>
> I coulda meet my death just so last night.
> If you did only lash she you woulda find out.
>
> 2.5.2 But Creole also uses **could have** and **would have** to refer to events which **did** happen. In other words Creole uses these as past simple tense verbs:
>
> That was the best one I coulda find.
> I didn't know you woulda come so early.
>
> We have seen that in Creole **could** and **would** are not past tense forms. Their past tense forms are **coulda** and **woulda** (i.e., **could have** and **would have**).

BEWARE! In Standard English **could have** and **would have** are NOT the past simple tense forms of **can** and **will**.

In English **could have** and **would have** are not used to refer to events which actually happened. This is wrong:

> X *I didn't fall asleep until about 2.00 a.m. because I <u>could have heard</u> the neighbours quarrelling.*

The speaker of this sentence obviously heard the neighbours quarrelling; but "could have heard" means that he or she **did not** hear.

X *You see? I told you it <u>would have rained.</u>*

Again this verb form indicates something that did not happen, but the gist of the sentence is that it **is** raining.

2.6 Both of these sentences refer to real events, or facts, and so the tense to be used is not the conditional but the past simple:

> I didn't fall asleep until about 2.00 a.m. because I **could hear** the neighbours quarrelling.
> You see? I told you it **would rain**.

2.7 Note well the make-up of the following verb phrases:

> **could + have** + past participle
> **would + have** + past participle
> **should + have** + past participle

2.7.1 The following are some very common errors:

> X *That pole could have <u>fell</u> on somebody.*
> X *That pole could have <u>fall</u> on somebody.*

Here the speakers have not used the past participle but the past *tense* form in one sentence and the bare form of the verb in the other.

> X *That pole could <u>of</u> fallen on somebody.*

Here **of** is used instead of **have**.
Sometimes double errors are committed:

> X *That pole could <u>of fell</u> on somebody.*
> X *That pole could <u>of fall</u> on somebody.*

These errors are made with all three verbs – **could, would** and **should**. The correct forms are:

> That pole could have fallen on somebody.
> That pole would have fallen on somebody.
> That pole should have fallen on somebody.

In speech these are contracted to:

> That pole **could've** fallen...
> That pole **would've** fallen...
> That pole **should've** fallen...

It is the sound of this shortened form **'ve** that some people mistake for **of**.

2.7.2 Question and negative forms are as follows:

Questions
Could that pole have fallen...?
Would that pole have fallen...?
Should that pole have fallen...?

Negative
That pole could not have fallen...
That pole would not have fallen...
That pole should not have fallen...

These are contracted to:

couldn't have/wouldn't have/shouldn't have

In informal speech these are contracted even further:

couldn't've/wouldn't've/shouldn't've

Negative questions (formal and contracted):

Could/would/should that pole not have fallen...?

Couldn't/wouldn't/shouldn/t that pole've fallen

Not only must we use these verb forms in the correct places, we must also be sure to construct them correctly.

STOP HERE AND DO F10 PRACTICE 4. – 7.

3. Requests and offers

Could and **would** are used for making polite requests and offers:

Could you move your car, please?
Would you like to try one of these?

NB: This is wrong:

X I <u>will</u> like to try one

The correct form in English is:

I **would** like to try one.

4. Would = used to

When we want to refer to actions which happened regularly in the past, we can place either **used to** or **would** before the verb:

> He used to go down to the waterfront every morning.
> He would go down to the waterfront every morning.

5. NB: Caribbean speakers often use would quite unnecessarily in English sentences, slipping it in where neither would nor will nor any other auxiliary is called for. In these situations, the form required is generally the present simple tense (see E4:2.3):

> X *On Sundays and public holidays there is no sanitation service and so the garbage <u>would pile</u> up on the pavements.*

This should be:

> On Sundays and public holidays there is no sanitation service and so the garbage piles up on the pavements.

DO F10 PRACTICE 8. – 10.

F10 Practice

1. Convert the following sentences into the past tense (see F10:1):
   (a) Rose thinks it will take too long.
   (b) They estimate that they can be at the airport by 5 o'clock.
   (c) You cannot register unless you pay the fee.
   (d) He says that there won't be another flight until late evening.
   (e) The suspect agrees to give himself up if the authorities will guarantee him a fair trial.

2. Convert the following sentences into the present tense (see F10:1):
   (a) In such an environment one could do as one pleased.
   (b) Nobody could understand what he meant.
   (c) We had no reason to doubt that the funds would be available.
   (d) That child could turn perfect cartwheels.
   (e) I had a feeling that it wouldn't work.

Past Simple Tense **F10**

3. Correct the errors of tense in the following sentences (see F10:1):

A. (a) *Show me one and I would tell you what it is.*
 (b) *Last night she made them turn off the TV so that they can study for their exams.*
 (c) *The notice also explained that the measure was temporary and that as soon as money was available, workers will be recalled.*
 (d) *A memorial service would be held for my great-aunt next Friday at 4.30 p.m.*
 (e) *The twins are so alike that the only people who could tell them apart are their family and close friends.*

B. (a) *I did not think they will go to such lengths.*
 (b) *If this continues the Caribbean would not develop its own identity and this can hinder social and economic growth.*
 (c) *Bishop warned Grenadians that an attack from the United States can come at any time.*
 (d) *The difficult situation we are in now would improve when more jobs become available.*
 (e) *Angela realized that the only person who can make her a professional artist was herself.*

4. Make sentences from this substitution table:

If	more people came forward	we could ensure a decent standard of living for everyone.
	we were all more cooperative	it would make a great difference.
	the businesspeople gave back a share of their profits to the community	we could solve the problems we face.
	everybody joined forces	our country would be a better place to live in.
	we refused to be divided by partisan politics	then there would be progress.
		we could achieve a high level of development.

5. Put a suitable modal auxiliary in each blank space: **will, would, can,** or **could** (See F10:2):
 (a) This gadget _____ function better if users followed the instructions for use.
 (b) If the Ministry does not take steps to reverse this trend, the education system in our country _____ rapidly deteriorate.
 (c) If the parent waited too long, the child _____ not understand why he or she was being corrected.

(d) The general health of the Caribbean population _____ improve if our governments became more serious about agriculture.

(e) If the efficient disposal of toxic wastes becomes mandatory in our legal systems, many industries throughout the world _____ face criminal action unless they comply with disposal laws.

6. Make sentences from this substitution table:

Without your help	we could not have done it.
Were it not for the dedication of members of staff	the programme would have collapsed.
If everybody had not worked very hard	there would have been no success story.
Without proper planning	we could not have made this dream a reality.
If we had not reached our fundraising target	the project would never have got off the ground.
	this venture could have ended in disaster.
	this undertaking would surely have failed.

7. For each empty slot, construct a suitable verb phrase, using the verb given with **could/would** or **could have/would have** (see F10:1 and 2):

For example, **to hear: could hear / would hear
could have heard / would have heard**

(a) It's a pity you were late, for if you had got there on time, you _____ them to the airport. (to take)

(b) As my eyes got accustomed to the darkness I _____ the features of the building. (to see)

(c) The phones were obviously down; otherwise he _____us when it happened. (to call)

(d) You obviously didn't study for this exam, or you _____. (to pass)

(e) The company promised that there _____ no further retrenchment. (to be)

8. Convert these sentences into polite requests or offers, using **could** or **would** (see F10:3):

(a) Put the food in the fridge.

(b) Take some of the flowers with you.

(c) Turn down that radio.

(d) File these letters before you go.

(e) Taste our rum punch.

9. Make sentences from this substitution table:

Whenever that person's name was mentioned	a hush would descend upon the gathering.
	his face would light up.
	people would tremble with fear.
	there would be loud cheering.
Every time he spoke	the younger ones would shriek with laughter.
	somebody would utter an obscenity.
In those days when such a thing happened	everbody would pay attention.
	she would relive the incident.
	my old aunt would cross herself.

10. In each of these sentences **would** has been used unnecessarily. Correct these errors (See F10:5)

   (a) *When you hire a guide to take you on one of the nature trails, he would tell you about the various animals and other points of interest.*

   (b) *Only candidates who are successful at this examination would qualify to do the practical examination.*

   (c) *Every Boxing Day we go to our aunt's house where we would eat lunch and play games.*

   (d) *As one gets older, one would need fewer calories per day.*

   (e) *There is a financial strain on the owner as the initial overhead expenses would be high.*

Answers pp. 266-267

G. The Past Participle

G1 IDENTIFYING THE PAST PARTICIPLE

1. (a) The group is selling **fried** chicken to raise funds.

    (b) We have **built** a day nursery in the village.

    (c) An election is **held** once every five years.

    The words in bold type above – **fried, built** and **held** – may look like past tense verbs, but they are not. They are **past participles.**

    The past participle is a form of the verb which usually looks the same as the past tense form – i.e., the verb takes on a **d, ed** or **t** ending.

2. However, in some verbs the past participle takes a different form from the past tense. These participles end with **n** or **en**, for example:

Infinitive	Past Tense	Past Participle
to give	gave	given
to take	took	taken

3. **In Creole, verbs do not change into a past participle form,** and so one of the errors that Caribbean people frequently make when they are using English is that they neglect to change the verb into its past participle form when necessary.

    X (d) *The Red Cross collects <u>use</u> clothing for hurricane victims.*

    X (e) *Our company has <u>receive</u> your application.*

    X (f) *Some people are <u>force</u> into a life of crime.*

    In order to use the English past participle correctly, you have to be aware of its uses. You have to know where it occurs.

4. **Where to find the past participle**

    You will find the past participle in three different roles.

    Look at sentences (a) to (f) above. First, let us correct sentences (d) to (f):

    (d) The Red Cross collects **used** clothing for hurricane victims.

    (e) Our company has **received** your application.

    (f) Some people are **forced** into a life of crime.

The Past Participle G1

Role No. 1: Adjective

In (a) the past participle **fried** describes **chicken.**
In (d) the same thing happens – **used** describes **clothing.**
In these two sentences, therefore, the past participle is used as an adjective. (See A3.)

Role No. 2: Perfect Tenses

In (b) and (e) the past participle is used with the auxiliary verb **to have.** Therefore the participle here is part of a verb phrase. Auxiliary and participle join together to form a verb in the **perfect tense.** There are many perfect tenses:

has received; had received; will have received; should have received, etc.

As you can see, each is a verb phrase made up of the past participle with a different tense of the verb **to have.** (See G3 and G4.)

Role No. 3: Passive Voice

In sentences (c) and (f) the past participle is used with another auxiliary: the verb **to be.** Together they form a verb in the passive voice (See G5). Again, the auxiliary can be in different tenses. All of the following are passive voice verbs:

is held; will be held; are being held; can be held, etc.

These are the three roles of the past participle, and in the sections following we shall look at each more closely.

G1 Practice

Identify the past participle in each of the sentences below.

1. *The past participle as an adjective*

   (a) It is inconsiderate to smoke in an enclosed area.

   (b) Houses built by the National Housing Authority are available at a lower cost.

   (c) The police found the car parked outside the stadium.

   (d) This text-book seems too advanced for the age-group.

   (e) They also believe that they are a chosen people.

2. *The perfect tenses*
Identify the past participle, and then underline the whole perfect tense verb phrase (i.e., auxiliary verb or verbs and past participle):

(a) I have seen this film twice.

(b) The rainy season had ended.

(c) It would have taken too long to rewrite.

(d) By the time the kettle boils, he will have made the sandwiches.

(e) The cost of living has risen steeply.

3. *The passive voice*
Identify the past participle and then underline the whole verb phrase:

(a) It is felt that the Treasurer should resign.

(b) Another community project will be undertaken in the new year.

(c) A sports meeting was organized by the Village Council.

(d) Two scholarships were offered this year.

(e) Nothing can be done about it at this stage.

Answers pp. 267-268

G2 THE PAST PARTICIPLE AS ADJECTIVE

1. **CREOLE GRAMMAR**

> **stew** beef
>
> **starch** clothes
>
> a boy **name** Gavin
>
> Mr Nathan get **vex**
>
> She come with she face well **paint** up.
>
> All the words in bold type here are verbs used as adjectives. They are all the bare form of the verb. In English these verbs would be in the past participle form. Creole does not require a change of form.
>
> In Standard English the bare form of the verb cannot be used as an adjective. It has to be changed into a participle. (For the present participle as adjective, see H1.)

2. Position

The past participle can be found in all the adjective positions shown in A9:5.

2.1 *Before the word modified*

Please find something for these **bored** children to do.

2.2 *As a subject complement*

The rape victim feels **degraded.**

See B5:1. When a past participle comes after **to be,** however, it is usually not an adjective. More often than not it is part of a verb phrase – **to be** + past participle – which is a passive voice verb. (See G5.)

In the following sentences the past participle is an adjective:

The house is **dilapidated** beyond recognition.
People were **interested** in every aspect of the case.

However, in the sentences below, **to be** and the past participle go together to form a verb phrase:

This building **was refurbished** last year.
Salaries **are paid** on the fourth Friday of the month.

2.3 *As an object complement*

They consider the report **exaggerated.**
See B5:2.

2.4 *Introduced by comparison word*

One child is as **disabled** as the other.

In addition, however, the past participle acting as an adjective can be found in the following positions:

2.5 *After the word modified*

Some past participles can follow the word modified – not only the direct object as in 2.3 above, but other nouns in the sentence:

The person **appointed** will have to report for duty on Monday.

The past participle in this position can be part of a phrase:

We must not forget the struggles **waged by our ancestors.**

2.6 Such a phrase can sometimes be placed before the word modified:

Taken by surprise, they had no choice but to surrender.

3. Nouns made into participles

3.1 Notice how names of parts of the body, which are really nouns, are used to form adjectives: they are turned into past participles.

long-haired, cross-eyed, dog-eared, flat-nosed, thin-lipped, left-handed, tight-fisted, pot-bellied, bow-legged, light-skinned

3.2 There are also other nouns (not parts of the body) which are used in this way. You have to be on the look-out for words such as these and remember to put on the "past participle" ending:

a three-storeyed house

a long-handled broom

the two-tiered rate of exchange

pin-striped cloth

a double-barrelled gun

3.3 Some words like these, however, do not take a past participle ending:

a double-decker bed

a three-bedroom house

a four-lane highway.

The "adjectives" here are really noun phrases: we have already seen (D4) how nouns can sometimes be used as adjectives (e.g., a football jersey).

3.4 Why should we say "a three-storeyed house", but a "a three-bedroom house"? There is no clear rule that can be given. This is one of those things that you simply have to pick up by reading widely and by consulting your dictionary when you are in doubt.

G2 Practice

1. A. The photograph shows a **barricaded** house.
   Replace **barricaded** with past participles made from the following verbs:
   (a) to ransack
   (b) to demolish
   (c) to paint
   (d) to fence
   (e) to decorate.

   B. The policies **imposed** by the new government were very unpopular.
   Replace **imposed** with past participles made from the following verbs:
   (a) to pursue
   (b) to implement
   (c) to outline
   (d) to adopt
   (e) to propose.

   C. Everybody in this house seems so **excited** these days.
   Replace **excited** with past participles made from the following verbs:
   (a) to irritate
   (b) to depress
   (c) to please
   (d) to occupy
   (e) to discourage

   D. The landlord wants the electricity supply **reconnected** by tomorrow.
   Replace **reconnected** with past participles made from the following verbs:
   (a) to disconnect
   (b) to regularize
   (c) to restore
   (d) to stabilize
   (e) to turn on

E. I am even more **exhausted** than you are.

Replace **exhausted** with past participles made from the following verbs:

(a) to impress

(b) to annoy

(c) to elate

(d) to disappoint

(e) to frustrate

2. Correct the past participle errors in the following sentences:

A. (a) *The knowledge gain in this exercise can be used to your advantage.*

(b) *She will eventually develop into an experience politician.*

(c) *This creature has a long, wedge-shape head.*

(d) *Now you look more puzzle than ever.*

(e) *A teacher who is punctual and discipline is less likely to have delinquent students.*

B. (a) *We did not cater for the increase inflow of tourists.*

(b) *My clothes stuck to my back and my hair resembled the feathers of a frizzle fowl.*

(c) *Some people see this practice as outdated and old-fashion.*

(d) *He does not possess the skills require for such a task.*

(e) *People going into self-employment should keep in mind the risks involve.*

C. (a) *Most letters to the editor are bias in favour of the ruling party.*

(b) *I am not surprise at all.*

(c) *You should be accustom to his manner by now.*

(d) *The Prime Minister agreed to meet with a delegation of concern residents.*

(e) *My mother is not too please with my results.*

3. The past participles that you have corrected at 2. above are all in the role of adjectives. Identify the word modified by each of these past participles.

Answers p. 268

G3 THE PRESENT PERFECT TENSE

1. Formation

1.1 The present perfect tense is formed as follows:

to have (present tense) + past participle.

(a) Mary has resigned.

(b) They have found a place to live.

The contracted forms are:

(a) Mary's resigned.

(b) They've found a place to live.

1.2 For the **question** form, subject and auxiliary are inverted, i.e., **to have** goes before its subject:

(a) Has Mary resigned?

(b) Have they found a place to live?

1.3 For the **negative** form, **not** is placed between auxiliary and participle:

(a) Mary has not resigned.

(b) They have not found a place to live.

These are contracted as follows:

(a) Mary hasn't resigned.

(b) They haven't found a place to live.

Be sure to put the apostrophe in the right place.

Beware of double negatives. (See E16.)

1.4 The present perfect requires **subject-verb agreement:** the auxiliary **to have** must agree with the subject. **Has** is used with third person singular subjects, and **have** with all others.

2. When to use the present perfect tense

Many Caribbean users of English are not sure when to use the present perfect tense. This is because Creole does not have a separate verb form that always corresponds exactly to this tense.

Caribbean people sometimes use the past simple tense (see F1) where the present perfect tense is required in English, and *vice versa:* the present perfect is sometimes mistakenly used where the past simple is the appropriate tense.

What is the difference between (a) "The house fell down" (past simple) and (b) "The house has fallen down" (present perfect)?

In sentence (a) the event is over and done with – the case is closed. In sentence (b) the event is still open – it is still fresh on our minds, still "news".

You use the present perfect tense if the action is *not* filed away in a closed time slot. You do not normally use this tense if the precise time of the action is stated in the sentence. This sentence is wrong:

> X *The house has fallen down last night.*

Usually, when a precise time or cut-off point is stated, the past simple tense is used:

> The house fell down last night.

With the present perfect tense there is no cut-off point: the time-frame remains open.

Even an action that took place years ago (even before we were born) can still be "open" or "fresh on our minds", i.e., we feel that the event is still alive and affecting the present, or the repercussions of that action are ongoing:

> I have lived through a war.
> Europe has plundered Africa without remorse.

3. CREOLE GRAMMAR

> In Creole, both English sentences
> > The house has fallen down (Present perfect), and
> > The house fell down (Simple past)
> would be rendered as
> > The house fall down.

> In fact, the bare form of the verb which in Creole serves as a general past tense verb is closer to the English present perfect than to the English past simple tense. (See also E15:3.2 and F6:2.)
>
> Sometimes when in Creole we add **did** to the verb, it is in order to show that we do not mean past "open" or recent, but past further back, over and done with. For example, if we say:
>
> > The dog and them **make** a hole in the fence.
>
> the hole could still be there, in which case an English speaker would use the present perfect:
>
> > The dogs **have made** a hole in the fence.
>
> If, however, the two neighbours on either side of the fence are now in court, ten months later when the case is finally called and when the bush that forms the fence has grown back and closed the hole, we are likely to say:
>
> > Them in courts because the dog and them **did make** a hole in the fence.
>
> For this an English speaker would use the past simple:
>
> > They are in court because the dogs **made** a hole in the fence.

4. You use the present perfect tense, more often than the past simple, with adverbs such as already, always, ever, just, never, recently, yet:

> I have just seen your mother.
> She has not yet returned my call.
> Have you ever smoked marijuana?

It is also used with adverbial phrases which indicate an ongoing past: "over the past few years", "up to news time", "since 1980".

5. The present perfect and its continuous form (see H2 and H3) are used to speak of actions or events that extend from the past into the present:

> She has lived there for years.
> She **has been living** there for years.
> They have fought among themselves since they were children.
> They **have been fighting** among themselves since they were children.

Note how the continuous form of the present perfect is put together. It has three parts:

> to have + **been** + present participle.

Been is the past participle of to **be.**

6. See G5 for the passive voice.

The passive voice verb phrase consists of the auxiliary verb **to be** and the past participle:

> We **were invited** to the ceremony. [Past simple tense]

This is a past simple tense verb because the auxiliary **to be** is in the past simple tense.

In the perfect tense this becomes:

> We **have been invited** to the ceremony.

The verb phrase then consists of:

> Perfect tense of **to be** + past participle.

7. NB: In American English you might hear the past simple tense used in places where British English would use the present perfect:

> Please come right away – your son broke his arm.

G3 Practice

1. Insert the form of the verb that is more appropriate – present perfect or past simple:

A. (a) I _____ the whole house already. (to clean)
   (b) On January 18th 1963, they _____ over to a new system. (to change)
   (c) Now, at long last, the Ministry of Education _____ a new Principal. (to appoint)
   (d) To date there _____ 99 murders this year. (to be)
   (e) She _____ to her grandchildren before she died. (to write)

B. The verbs in the following sentences must be in the passive voice (see G3:6 above). Choose the present perfect or the past simple:

   (a) Latest reports are that the missing children _____. (to find)
   (b) Only half of the money _____ so far. (to collect)
   (c) The bridges _____ in the dry season. (to repair)

(d) Some new measures _____ since the last meeting. (to introduce)

(e) Yesterday he _____ somewhere in the vicinity of Tacarigua. (to see)

2. Begin each of these sentences with the phrase given, changing the verb from the past simple to the present perfect. For example:

> Over the past few months...
>> They consumed gallons of alcohol.
>
> Over the past few months they have consumed gallons of alcohol.

A. Over the past few months...

(a) He lost a lot of weight.

(b) The two families were involved in a bitter land dispute.

(c) Attendance fell off considerably.

(d) More than 50 vendors' stalls were demolished.

(e) It rained almost every day.

B. Since the opening of the new highway...

(a) The public transport system improved considerably.

(b) The tranquillity of the countryside was destroyed.

(c) Whole villages sprang up in that part of the island.

(d) Road fatalities rose dramatically.

(e) Rural and urban communities were brought closer together.

3. Complete these sentences with the present perfect continuous form of the verb given. For example:

> The cat _____ all day. (to sleep)
> The cat has been sleeping all day.

(a) They _____ in line outside the U.S. Embassy since four o'clock this morning. (to stand)

(b) For the past 30 minutes the operator _____ to connect me. (to try)

(c) It's hard to believe that she _____ in that store for three months already. (to work)

(d) I _____ you all along. (to watch)

(e) For as long as I can remember, Miss Olive _____ stray dogs in the district. (to feed)

Answers pp. 268-269

G4 THE PAST PERFECT TENSE

1. Formation

1.1 The past perfect tense (also known as the pluperfect tense) is formed as follows: **had** + past participle.

> Farmers **had cleared** the land.

Had is the past tense of **to have.**

1.2 Passive voice verbs (see G5) in the past perfect tense are formed as follows: **had been** + past participle.

> The land **had been cleared** by farmers.

Had been is the past perfect tense of **to be.**

2. Further back than past tense

(a) When we **got** to the airport the plane *had left.*

(b) The house **had burnt** to the ground by the time the Fire Services **responded.**

(c) People **were fleeing** the city in panic, for rebel forces *had overthrown* the government.

In each of these sentences there are verbs in two different tenses.

In (a) and (b) one verb is in the past simple and the other in the past perfect tense.

In (c) one verb is in the past continuous tense (see H2) and the other in the past perfect tense.

The past perfect verbs are in italics.

In each sentence, the past perfect verb goes further back in time than the other verb. When we are recounting events or situations in the past tense (past simple or past continuous) we sometimes need to show that some past actions were completed before others. When we are talking about a time that is past but need to look further back from there, we use the past perfect tense.

With sentence (a), for example, a different meaning would be conveyed if both verbs were in the past simple tense:

> When we **got** to the airport the plane **left.**

In this sentence, the events happen in a different order. With both verbs in the past simple tense, we understand that the plane left right *after* the speaker's arrival at the airport. In sentence (a) above, however, the past perfect tense (**had left**) tells us that the plane took off *before* the speaker's arrival at the airport.

3. Reported speech

(d) Neighbours **told** the police that they **had seen** a young man prowling around the house two days before the fire.

(e) Mr Gordon **was saying** that his firm **had contributed** enough to the sports club.

In these sentences the clauses which contain the past perfect are *reported speech*.

3.1 To give an account of something a person has said, we either repeat the exact words spoken (direct speech), or we present a report of what was said (indirect speech, or reported speech).

When direct speech is written, it is enclosed in quotation marks " ":

(f) "We saw a young man prowling around the house two days before the fire", neighbours told the police.

(g) "My firm has contributed enough to the sports club", Mr Gordon was saying.

When speech is reported, quotation marks are not used, and certain changes are made to the speakers' original words. One of these changes may be **tense**.

Sentence (d) above is sentence (f) with the direct speech converted into reported speech; and sentence (e) is (g) with the direct speech reported.

Reported speech is usually introduced by a clause with what we might call a "reporting verb" such as **to say, to reply, to shout.**

3.2 If this reporting verb is in the present tense, then the tenses of the original speech are not changed:

Neighbours **tell** us that they **saw** a young man prowling around the house two days before the fire.

Mr Gordon **is saying** that his firm **has contributed** enough to the sports club.

3.3 If the verbs in direct speech are in the past tense or the present perfect [as in (f) and (g) above], and the reporting verb is in the past tense, then the verbs in the reported-speech clause must be in the past perfect tense:

Direct speech	*Reported speech*
(f) saw	(d) had seen
(g) has contributed	(e) had contributed

3.4 However, if the verbs in direct speech are in the present tense, then they are turned into the past tense (not the past perfect) when the reporting verb is in the past tense.

Direct speech

"I **am seeing** a young man prowling around the house", the neighbour told police.

"My firm **contributes** enough to the sports club", Mr Gordon was saying.

Reported speech

The neighbour told police that she **was seeing** a young man prowling around the house.

Mr Gordon was saying that his firm **contributed** enough to the sports club.

4. Sequence of tenses

When a narration moves between different points in time, the tenses we use must show this. We must choose the right **sequence of tenses.**

4.1 We have seen how in a past tense narration we need to express "older" events in the past perfect tense:

My aunt **insisted** that the electrician ***had stolen*** her money.

People **were fleeing** the city in panic, for rebel forces ***had overthrown*** the government.

4.2. If, however, we are narrating events in the present tense, then to go further back in time we do not need the past perfect. In such sentences, older events are expressed in the past simple, or the present perfect for the recent or "open" past (see G3:2):

My aunt **insists** that the electrician **stole** her money.

People **are fleeing** the city in panic, for rebel forces **have overthrown** the government.

4.3 In the sequence of tenses, the present perfect is not so straightforward. The present perfect tense hovers between past and present (see G3:2).

4.3.1 As we have seen, present perfect verbs in direct speech are changed into the past perfect in reported speech, when the reporting verb is in the past tense. (See 3.3 above.) This means that the present perfect is then treated as a past tense:

DIRECT SPEECH: "My firm **has contributed** enough to the sports club."

REPORTED SPEECH: Mr Gordon was saying that his firm **had contributed** enough to the sports club.

4.3.2 HOWEVER, when it is the reporting verb that is in the present perfect, or when we narrate events in the present perfect, this tense is treated like the present tense. Just as in 4.2 above, older events are *not* expressed in the past perfect, but in the past simple [(a) + (b) below], or the present perfect [(c) + (d) below].

(a) My aunt **has insisted** all along that the electrician **stole** her money.
(b) Neighbours **have told** the police that they **saw** a young man prowling around the house two days before the fire.
(c) People **have fled** the city in panic, for rebel forces **have overthrown** the government.
(d) We **have** just **learnt** that the price of oil **has fallen.**

5. Errors

5.1 Be on the lookout for situations which require the past perfect. These two sentences are wrong:

X *The office was in such a state that they knew thieves <u>broke</u> in.*

X *When our reporter visited the area after the flood she learnt that the water also <u>destroyed</u> livestock.*

Each of these sentences recounts events or situations that occurred at two different periods in the past. However, because all the verbs are in the past simple tense, it seems as though everything happened at the same time, or the actions took place one after the other, in a straight row. That is not the case.

In each sentence there is one action that preceded the others. That action must be expressed in the past perfect tense, since the others, the more recent ones, are expressed in the past simple:

The office **was** in such a state that they **knew** thieves *had broken* in.
When our reporter **visited** the area after the flood she **learnt** that the water *had* also *destroyed* livestock.

5.2 On the other hand, *do not* use the past perfect tense when there is no need to. These sentences are wrong:

X *Last month the Minister of Labour <u>had announced</u> his resignation.*

X *We are here because the foreman <u>had advised</u> us to report for work today.*

In the first of these two sentences, only one event is mentioned. There is no other past event that it precedes. Only one period of time in the past is involved. Therefore the tense to be used is the past simple:

Last month the Minister of Labour **announced** his resignation.

In the following sentence, however, the use of the past perfect is correct:

> By the end of February the Minister of Labour **had announced** his resignation.

Here the end of February is an event in the past, and we are looking back at the Minister's resignation from that point in the past.

In the second incorrect sentence above, there are two events, and one is more recent than the other. However, the more recent event is not expressed in a past tense verb. It is expressed in a present tense verb: **are**. The speaker is looking back from the present, not from a point in the past. For the older event, therefore, the past simple tense must be used:

> We are here because the foreman **advised** us to report for work today.

If we were to change the present tense verb to the past tense, then we would use the past perfect tense for the older event:

> We **were** there because the foreman ***had advised*** us to report for work on that day.

5.3 When Creole speakers use the English past perfect instead of the past simple, it may be that they are looking for a tense that matches the Creole past tense formed with **did**. See G3:3.

As we have seen, however, the English and Creole verb systems are different, and Creole verb forms do not always have an exact match in English.

The different "degrees of pastness" that Creole verb forms express are not always quite the same as those expressed by the English present perfect, past simple and past perfect. Creole speakers have to learn to separate these three English tenses, and this is one of those things which cannot be learnt out of any rule-book. Reading widely will help you to master the English verb system.

6. If-clauses

For the use of the past perfect in if-clauses, or conditional sentences, see F10:2.3.

G4 Practice

1. Make sentences from this substitution table.

Nobody knew People were discovering They realized then It was not clear to us The news report revealed	that why	Brazil had won the match. the Pageant had been postponed. their plan had backfired. some of the staff had already been transferred. food prices had increased by ten percent. she had left the job. these laws had been amended.

2. Convert the following sentences to the passive voice. (See **G5 Practice** 1.) For example:

   Farmers had cleared the land.

       The land had been cleared by farmers.

   (a) Rebel forces had overthrown the government.

   (b) They had seen a young man prowling around the house two days before the fire.

   (c) The electrician had stolen her money.

   (d) The water had also destroyed livestock.

   (e) The foreman had advised us to report for work on that day.

3. Fill each empty slot with the correct tense of the verb given – past or past perfect:

   (a) The maxi-taxi driver went straight to the police station to report that he and his passengers _____ robbed by bandits. (to be)

   (b) Our dog disappeared one morning but _____ just before nightfall. (to reappear).

   (c) The child was taken to Ward 14 where he _____ about twenty other abandoned children. (to join)

   (d) She nearly fainted when she was told that she _____ the jackpot. (to win)

   (e) When they _____ enough they got back into their cars and drove off. (to see)

4. Convert the following sentences into reported speech (see G4:3):

   (a) "The Ministry of Works spent thousands of dollars on widening the Cumana Road", Mr Singh replied.

   (b) "Those children waste too much water", Brian complained.

(c) "Only one of the Siamese twins has survived the operation", the bulletin states.

(d) "She did it just to tease her boyfriend", her brother explained.

(e) "Flight 327 is already boarding", the counter clerk announced.

Answers p. 269

G5 THE PASSIVE VOICE

1. (a) Cynthia stores the vaccines in a refrigerator.

   (b) The vaccines are stored (by Cynthia) in a refrigerator.

   The two sentences have more or less the same meaning. They are, however, constructed differently.

   Identify the subject, verb and object (if any) of each sentence.

   In (a) the subject is **Cynthia,** the verb **stores,** and **vaccines** the object.

   In (b) **vaccines** is the subject and the verb is **are stored.**

   In (b) there is no object in the normal sense. The object of the action stands in the subject position.

   The verb is also different in sentence (b). It is made up as follows:

   > **to be** + past participle

   Sentence (a) is the more usual way of constructing sentences. This sentence is in the "active voice" – it has an active subject. The subject carries out the action of the verb.

   Sentence (b) is in the "passive voice". Its subject is said to be passive, because it is acted upon. It does not act.

2. **The passive construction is used when we wish to focus attention on the object of an action rather than on the doer of the action.** The doer, if mentioned at all, is placed in a prepositional phrase – the doer becomes the object of the preposition **by**. However, in passive voice sentences it is not always necessary to mention the doer:

   > The vaccines are stored in a refrigerator.
   > Beer is made from hops.

3. **Note that only transitive verbs (see B3:4) can be turned into the passive voice.** Verbs which do not take objects cannot be made passive, because it is objects that become subjects in the passive voice.

The subject of a passive voice sentence can be either a direct or an indirect object (see B4). Let us take the following sentence which has a direct and an indirect object:

> They sent the firm a letter of protest.

This sentence can be turned into the passive voice in two ways:

> A letter of protest was sent to the firm. (Direct object turned into subject)
>
> The firm was sent a letter of protest. (Indirect object turned into subject)

4. **Different tenses of the passive voice are formed by varying the tense of the auxiliary verb to be, for example:**

> The vaccines **are** stored in a refrigerator.
> The vaccines **were** stored...
> The vaccines **are being** stored...
> The vaccines **had been** stored...

The passive voice may also be formed with modals (see E18:1.2):

> The vaccines **can** be stored...
> The vaccines **should** be stored...
> The vaccines **must** have been stored...

NB: Only the auxiliary varies in form. For all tenses of the passive voice the main verb is in the past participle form.

5. **Subject-verb agreement is required for some tenses of the passive voice.**

There is no subject-verb agreement when the verb phrase begins with a modal (see 4. above). However, when the verb phrase begins with **to be** in the present or past tense, or **to have** in the present tense, that auxiliary verb has to agree with the subject:

> The food is stored...
> The vaccines were stored...
> The food is being stored...
> The vaccines are being stored...
> The food has been stored...
> The vaccines have been stored...

6. **The question and negative forms of the passive voice are really the question and negative forms of the verb to be followed by the main verb:**

> Are the vaccines stored...?
> Have the vaccines been stored...?
> The vaccines may not be stored...
> Weren't the vaccines stored...?

7. **CREOLE GRAMMAR**

> In Creole passive voice sentences, as in English, the object of the action is the subject of the sentence.
>
> Where Creole differs from English, however, is that the form of the verb is the same for active as for passive voice sentences:
>
> **Trinidadian**
>
> | | |
> |---|---|
> | *Present tense:* | The floor **does mop** every day. |
> | *Past tense:* | The floor **mop** yesterday. |
> | *Future tense:* | The floor **go mop** tomorrow. |
> | *With modals:* | The floor **can mop** now. |
>
> **Jamaican**
>
> | | |
> |---|---|
> | *Present tense:* | The floor **mop** every day. |
> | *Past tense:* | The floor **did mop** yesterday. |
> | *Future tense:* | The floor **going mop** tomorrow. |
> | *With modals:* | The floor **can mop** now. |

8. **Creole speakers sometimes carry over the Creole passive voice into English, using an active voice verb form. This is incorrect:**

> X *Renovations to the airport can postpone to next year.*

> The correct form of the verb in this sentence is: **can be postponed**

9. **When using the passive voice in English, we should also pay special attention to the following:**

   – Subject-verb agreement.

   – The past participle form of the main verb.

   – The difference between **being** and **been**. (See H3.)

These are some common errors:

> X Looters in the city <u>was</u> shot at by soldiers.
>
> X The pain can be <u>relieve</u> by medication.
>
> X A calypso competition has <u>being</u> organized as part of the Independence celebrations.

The correct forms are:

> Looters in the city **were** shot at by soldiers.
>
> The pain can be **relieved** by medication.
>
> A calypso competition has **been** organized as part of the Independence celebrations.

10. **In trying to use the passive voice, people sometimes go overboard and produce wrong constructions such as these:**

> X (a) Stricter measures <u>are needed to be implemented</u>
>
> X (b) Sex education <u>should be continued to be taught</u>.
>
> X (c) Prices <u>have been tried to be reduced</u>.

10.1 In each of these sentences the verb phrase is made up of two verbs. In (a) and (b) there is no reason for the first verb to be in the passive voice. The correct forms of (a) and (b) are:

> Stricter measures **need to be implemented.**
> Sex education **should continue to be taught.**

As for sentence (c), "to try to do" simply cannot be made passive, and so the idea has to be expressed in an active voice sentence:

> They **have tried to reduce** prices.

10.2 The sentence patterns attempted in (a) to (c) above need some attention. There are actually three types which involve the passive voice;

> (d) Stricter measures **need to be implemented.**
>
> (e) That man **is known to have been deported** from the United States.
>
> (f) These flowers **are said to possess** healing qualities.

These verb phrases are constructed as follows:

> (d) active voice finite verb + passive voice infinitive

(e) passive voice finite verb + passive voice infinitive

(f) passive voice finite verb + active voice infinitive

10.3 Only a certain set of verbs can be used as the first verb in this kind of verb phrase. Some of the verbs most commonly used in pattern (d) are:

to want, to have, to need, to continue, to be, to seem

For patterns (e) and (f) the first verb is usually one of the following:

to say, to know, to think, to believe, to show, to deem

10.4 In these patterns the use of tenses needs special attention.

10.4.1 Infinitives have basically two tenses – present and perfect.

In the **active voice** these are:

PRESENT: to write
PERFECT: to have written

In the **passive voice** these are:

PRESENT: to be written
PERFECT: to have been written

In the patterns (d)–(f) above, the second verb (the infinitive) is sometimes present and sometimes perfect.

10.4.2 If the two verbs refer to situations or events going on at the same time, then the second verb is in the present tense, whatever the tense of the first verb:

Devices such as these **are known to be used** in the manufacture of home-made guns.

Devices such as these **were known to be used** in the manufacture of home-made guns.

10.4.3 However, if the second verb goes further back in time than the first, then that second verb is in the perfect tense:

That man **is known to have been deported** from the US.
The situation **was said to have deteriorated.**

G5 Practice

1. Convert the following sentences into the passive voice. If the subject of the original sentence is important to the meaning of the sentence, it may be expressed in a "by" phrase, for example:

   Village Councils maintain all recreational facilities.
   All recreational facilities are maintained by Village Councils.

   If this subject is not essential to meaning, it may be omitted. For example:

   The two parties settled the matter out of court.
   The matter was settled out of court.

A. (a) People all over the world admire his work.

   (b) The school provides meals for underprivileged children.

   (c) We expect her to arrive tomorrow.

   (d) Their political allegiance always influences their judgement in these matters.

   (e) Residents leave bags of garbage everywhere.

B. (a) The government put a limited area of the country under curfew.

   (b) They built their houses entirely out of indigenous materials.

   (c) A new and little-known calypsonian took the crown this year.

   (d) Doctors pronounced two of the accident victims dead on arrival.

   (e) The man released the hostages one by one to a waiting crowd.

C. (a) Competition between the two breweries has lowered the price of beer.

   (b) By then they had already published the results of the Common Entrance Examination.

   (c) Our people will remember these events for a long time to come.

   (d) Nothing can justify this expense.

   (e) The subcommittee must present an emergency plan within twenty-four hours.

2. Replace the part of each sentence in bold type with verb phrases of the same pattern, formed with the verbs given, for example:

   Stricter measures need **to be implemented**. (to adopt)
   Stricter measures need **to be adopted**.

   A. These buildings need **to be cleaned**.

(a) to inspect
(b) to repair
(c) to paint
(d) to renovate
(e) to spray.

B. Workers continue **to be retrenched** by the company.
(a) to fire
(b) to hire
(c) to redeploy
(d) to victimize
(e) to recruit

C. Nothing seems **to have been taken.**
(a) to do
(b) to decide
(c) to move
(d) to disturb
(e) to change

D. At least one hundred of these are known **to be sold** every week.
(a) to steal
(b) to import
(c) to destroy
(d) to distribute
(e) to produce

E. The priests **were believed** to have harboured a fugitive.
(a) to think
(b) to say
(c) to know
(d) to allege
(e) to report

3. Correct the errors in the following sentences.

A. (a) *The staging of fetes and the playing of sound systems in residential areas cannot be condone.*
(b) *The economic hardships which are at present experiencing by all Caribbean countries are the result of Structural Adjustment.*
(c) *Young children are needed to be corrected at the very instant of their wrongdoing.*
(d) *It is obvious that people's lives has been changed.*
(e) *The statistics of crime will only be reduce if we attack the root causes.*

B. (a) *This problem should rectified possibly by the proper training of teachers.*
(b) *The conditions of colonialism may persist long after independence have been gained.*
(c) *On your driving test hand signals are asked to be demonstrated and a hill test asked to be done.*
(d) *This, it is hoped, will put a halt to the decline that is being experience at the present moment.*
(e) *Over the years calypsonians kept going back and looking for songs that could recycle.*

C. (a) *Any measure which brings such hardship to working people should be abandon immediately.*
(b) *The rules state that students not suppose to wear jewelry to school.*
(c) *His enemies will not satisfy until they see him fail.*
(d) *These vehicles are very badly maintain.*
(e) *A young child can be depress by any number of things.*

Answers pp. 269-270

G6 NOTABLE PAST PARTICIPLES

1. Verbs which do not change

See F2.

1.1 The past participle of **to beat** is **beaten.** This verb is an exception among those listed in F2. All the others have the same form for the past participle as for the infinitive.

1.2 There are three other common verbs that do not change for the past participle. These verbs change for the **past tense** (unlike those in F2) but their past participle is the same as their basic form (infinitive):

Infinitive	Past Tense	Past Participle
to come	came	come
to become	became	become
to run	ran	run

1.3 Here is a list of all the common verbs that have the same form in the past participle as in the infinitive:

become	come	hurt	shut
bet	cost	let	split
broadcast	cut	put	spread
burst	forecast	run	
cast	hit	set	

2. NB: "Read" and "lead"

2.1 The past participle of **to read,** like its past tense, is written **read**; but it is pronounced "red".

2.2 However, the past tense and past participle forms of **to lead** are pronounced AND WRITTEN **led:**

> Mother Irene led the delegation.
>
> His response has led us to believe that he is sincere.

People often write **lead** for the past participle form of **to lead.** This is incorrect.

The word that is written **lead** and pronounced "led" refers to the metal:

> This thing is as **heavy as lead.**

3. I-A-U Verbs

3.1 Look at the pattern in these verbs:

Infinitive	Past Tense	Past Participle
begin	began	begun
drink	drank	drunk
ring	rang	rung
shrink	shrank	shrunk
sing	sang	sung
sink	sank	sunk
swim	swam	swum

These verbs all have **i** in their basic form, and this changes to **a** for the past tense and **u** for the past participle.

3.2 The problem that occurs here is that people switch around the past tense and past participle forms:

> X *As soon as they arrived on the site, they <u>begun</u> to work.*
>
> X *Our profits have <u>sank</u> to an all-time low.*

Be on the look-out for these verbs, and be sure to choose the correct forms – **a** for the past tense and **u** for the past participle:

As soon as they arrived on the site, they **began** to work.

Our profits have **sunk** to an all-time low.

4. "Lay" and "lie"

4.1 In Standard English **to lay** is a transitive verb, which is to say that it takes a direct object (see B3). You can't just "lay" – you have to lay something:

> (a) Will you please lay the table.
>
> (b) A mason lays bricks row by row.

(When we say "The hens are laying", the object **eggs** is understood.)

4.2 "To lie" is intransitive. You don't lie anything; you just lie. The verb has two different meanings:

> (c) I lie in my bed for hours reading.
>
> (d) Dishonest people lie, cheat and steal.

The sentences above contain the present tense forms of **to lay** [(a) and (b)] and **to lie** [(c) and (d)].

4.3 Creole uses **lay** as **lie** is used in sentence (c) above.

> "I does lay down in my bed."

So do some British and American non-standard dialects:

> "I think I'll just lay here for a while."

4.4 The past tense and past participle forms of these verbs present problems for users of English all over the world. People everywhere are liable to get them hopelessly mixed up.

We are dealing here with three different verbs:

1. **to lay** as in sentences (a) and (b) above.

2. **to lie** as in sentence (c) above.

3. **to lie** as in sentence (d) above.

Infinitive	Past Tense	Past Participle
1. to lay	laid	laid [put down]
2. to lie	lay	lain [rest]
3. to lie	lied	lied [tell untruth]

For example:

1. (a) He **laid** his hand on my shoulder.

   (b) We have **laid** new vinyl on the kitchen floor.

2. (a) Their belongings **lay** on the pavement.

   (b) It was obvious that she had **lain** in bed all day.

3. (a) They **lied** about their age in order to be allowed into the nightclub.

   (b) This is not the first time that this child has **lied** to me.

5. **CREOLE GRAMMAR**

> There are a few verbs that Creole has taken from English in their past participle form. That is to say that the English participle is used in Creole as the basic form:
>
> Some people does **married** for money.
>
> She have nowhere else to **left** she children.
>
> He go **lost** all he money in the wappie again.

In English the basic forms of the Creole verbs above are **to marry, to leave, to lose**. However, when Creole usage is carried over into English, we get errors such as these:

X *You cannot just left your job like that.*

X *She is not too eager to married anybody.*

X *If we lost our bus fare again, we will have to walk.*

In English the correct forms are:

You cannot just **leave** your job like that.
She is not too eager to **marry** anybody.
If we **lose** our bus fare again, we will have to walk.

6. Lost-Loss-Lose-Loose

The English verb **to lose** needs special attention. It is often confused with **loss** and **loose**.

6.1 Creole speakers may tend to confuse the English words **lost, lose, loss** and **loose** for reasons of pronunciation.

>The verb that means **to lose** in Creole (see 5. above) is pronounced "lorse". It comes from the English **lost,** but in the Creole there is no **t** sound at the end.
>
>The noun **loss** is also pronounced "lorse" in Creole. In written English, therefore, some people mix up **lost, lose** and **loss**.
>
>The English verb **lose** is pronounced "looze": it has the same vowel sound as **loose**. Therefore people sometimes write **loose** for **lose**.

The sentences below show how these words are used in English:

6.2 To lose

>Try not to **lose** your bus fare again. (Infinitive)
>You **lose** your bus fare too often. (Present simple)
>Henry **loses** his bus fare regularly. (Present simple)
>He **lost** his bus fare on the playing-field. (Past simple)
>Henry has **lost** his bus fare again. (Past participle)

6.3 Loss

Loss is not a verb. It is a noun:
>The company suffered a great **loss** that year.

6.4 Loose

>Nobody can set foot in that yard when the dogs are **loose**. (Adjective)

Loose is used most often as an adjective, but it can also be a verb:

>It is time to **loose** the dogs. (Infinitive)
>They **loose** the dogs at night. (Present simple)
>Freda **loosed** the dogs at 7.00 p.m. (Past simple)
>Somebody has already **loosed** the dogs. (Past participle)

6.5 Then there is **loosen** which is **not** the past participle of **to loose**. **Loosen** is a verb formed by adding **en** to the adjective **loose** (see G7:2). It has its own past participle: **loosened**.

Consult your dictionary to be clear about how these verbs differ in meaning:

Infinitive	Past Tense	Past Participle
to lose	lost	lost
to loose	loosed	loosed
to loosen	loosened	loosened

G6 Practice

1. Convert these sentences into the passive voice. (See **G5 Practice** 1.)
   (a) Vendors lay out all kinds of goods on the pavement.
   (b) The Principal runs the school like a military operation.
   (c) We sing the National Anthem at all public functions.
   (d) In this game competitors lose five points for each incorrect response.
   (e) Between 3.00 and 3.15 p.m. the radio station broadcasts government notices.

2. Convert these sentences into the present perfect tense. (See G3.)
   (a) Structural Adjustment policies lead to an increase in poverty.
   (b) This mirror never lies.
   (c) Patients lie here for hours with no one to attend to them.
   (d) New musical forms begin to appear.
   (e) The bell rings to signal the end of a session.

Answers p. 271

G7 VERBS ENDING WITH *D*, *T*, OR *EN*

1. See F4.

The same mistake is made with the past participle: verbs ending with a **d** or **t** sound tend to be used, unchanged, for past participle forms:

> X *The Chamber of Commerce has <u>applaud</u> what it sees as a wise move on the part of the government.*

This should be:

> *The Chamber of Commerce has* **applauded**...

2. There is another group of words, however, that people mistakenly use as past participle forms.

   2.1 Because some verbs take on the ending **en** for their past participle form, verbs which already end with this sound are sometimes used unchanged, for the past participle:

   X *This woman is always <u>burden</u> with work.*

   The correct form is:

   This woman is always **burdened** with work.

   2.2 The error is made especially with verbs that are formed by adding the suffix **en** to other words, for example:

broad	+	en	=	broaden
red	+	en	=	redden
worse	+	en	=	worsen
threat	+	en	=	threaten
fright	+	en	=	frighten

   The suffix **en** in this case is not a past participle ending. **Broad, red** and **worse** are adjectives; **threat** and **fright** are nouns. The suffix **en** is added to turn them into verbs. These **en** words are infinitives (see A4:3). For their past participle form we have to add **ed**, for example:

   Conditions have **worsened** over the past year.

G7 Practice

1. Convert the following sentences into the passive voice (**see G5 Practice 1**):
   (a) They treat their machinery with great care.
   (b) Some masqueraders frighten little children.
   (c) We regard your statement as an ultimatum.
   (d) Such events sadden our hearts.
   (e) The older people reject these sudden changes.

2. Convert the following sentences into the present perfect tense (see G3):
   (a) Participants adopt a cautious attitude.
   (b) The landlord often threatens his tenants with eviction.
   (c) Mildew blackens the walls of the hospital.
   (d) This new development actually strengthens our position.
   (e) Talks between the two parties inevitably end on a sour note.

3. Correct the past participle errors in the following sentences:
   (a) *People were being affect by noise.*
   (b) *It was obvious that their situation had worsen since the onset of the dry season.*
   (c) *Our knowledge has been broaden by this experience.*
   (d) *The company has also build schools.*
   (e) *Your water supply will be disconnect if you don't pay the bill.*

Answers p. 271

H. The Present Participle

H1 THE PRESENT PARTICIPLE AS NOUN AND ADJECTIVE

1. **The present participle is the form of the verb which ends with ing.** It can be part of a verb phrase (see H2); it can act as a noun; and it can act as an adjective.

   Even when it acts as a noun or an adjective, however, the present participle continues to behave in some ways like a verb:

   – When it acts as a noun it can have an object.

   – When it acts as an adjective it can have a subject or an object.

2. **As a noun**

   Present participles acting as nouns (sometimes called **gerunds**) can be found in all the regular noun slots (see A9):

   ### 2.1 With determiners:

   2.1.1 A present participle in a noun slot is usually an uncountable noun, so more often then not it will have no article **(a/an, the)** before it (see C5 and C6):

   > **Smoking** is an unhealthy habit.
   > The driver was fined for **speeding.**

   2.1.2 Like other uncountable nouns, it may be used with the definite article **the:**

   > **The smoking** of cigarettes is prohibited.
   > Stop **the speeding.**

   2.1.3 Uncountable nouns are not normally used with the indefinite article (**a/an**). There are, however, some present participles which have come to be used as countable nouns as well as uncountable nouns. These can therefore be used with **a/an,** and they can also be made plural. Here are a few of them:

a beating	-	beatings
a building	-	buildings
a killing	-	killings
a screening	-	screenings
a wedding	-	weddings

   2.1.4 Present participles acting as nouns are used with other determiners as well:

no dumping; this fighting; your coming; June's singing

2.2 **With adjectives:**

good cooking

2.3 *As object of a preposition:*

by saving

2.4 **With There + to be:**

There will be dancing in the streets.

2.5 *As subject of a verb:*

Walking improves the circulation.

2.6 *As object of a verb:*

They have legalized gambling.

3. A present participle acting as a noun can be the head of a noun phrase, like any other noun (see E6:1). Here are some noun phrases in which the head word is a present participle:

regular **eating** in restaurants
any loud **playing** of music
accounting for money spent
the **writing** of a book

4. Unlike other nouns, however, a present participle acting as a noun can have a direct object (see B3). Many noun phrases are formed in this way. Here the direct objects are in italics:

driving a sleek *car*
taking his *time*
killing two *birds* with one stone
making your *presence* felt

5. As an adjective

The present participle acting as an adjective may also either stand on its own:

(a) **Rising** prices have created great hardship. (Word modified: **prices**)

(b) The person **calling** wants to leave a message for Mr Lee Lum. (Word modified: **person)**

or it may be the head word of a phrase – an adjective phrase:

(c) Passengers **claiming their baggage** must join this queue. (Word modified:

passengers)

   (d) **Taking one last look around the room,** she closed the door and left. (Word modified: **she**).

6. **Remember that the present participle is really a verb form,** so it may have "subjects" and "objects":

   6.1 In each of the sentences above, the word modified can also be seen as a kind of subject of the present participle. **Rising** is an action performed by **prices,** and so on. Understanding this relationship will help you to understand and avoid the error of sentence structure known as a "dangling modifier" (dealt with in Level 2 of this manual).

   6.2 In sentences (c) and (d) above, the present participle has an object as well. In (c) **baggage** is the object of **claiming,** and in (d) **look** is the object of **taking.**

7. **Like the infinitive (see G5:10.4.1) the present participle has a present tense and a perfect tense.**

   In the active voice these are:

   > PRESENT: writing
   > PERFECT: having written

   The passive voice forms are:

   > PRESENT: being written
   > PERFECT: having been written

   The **perfect tense form** is used when the participle refers to a previous action:

   > **Having claimed their baggage,** the passengers joined the Customs queue. (Word modified: **passengers**)

   Sometimes the **passive voice** (see G5) is required:

   > **Having been robbed twice,** he wanted to install a security system. (Word modified: **he**)

8. **Noun or adjective?**

   How can you tell whether a present participle is acting as a noun or as an adjective, when the same word or phrase can play either role?

   (a) I will not tolerate this endless **bickering.**

   (b) **Bickering** children are a nuisance.

The Knots In English

(c) **Driving a sleek car** is his idea of success.

(d) A young man **driving a sleek car** came to see you yesterday.

As with any other word or phrase, one has to look at what role it plays in the sentence. What is its relationship to other words in the sentence?

In (a) **bickering** is the object of the verb. It therefore fills a noun slot.

In (b) the same word modifies **children,** so here it is an adjective.

In (c) the phrase in bold type is the subject of the verb, and is therefore a noun phrase.

In (d) the same phrase modifies **man,** and this makes it an adjective.

H1 Practice

1. Fill each of these noun slots with a suitable present participle:

    (a) Three of them have been arrested for _____ a man.

    (b) _____ this exam is all he can think about at the moment.

    (c) I do not think that _____ will help.

    (d) She doesn't mind cooking, but she really hates _____.

    (e) If I had the time, I would sign up for a course in _____.

2. Fill each of these adjective slots with a suitable present participle:

    (a) The boy _____ up the road is Miss Pauline's son.

    (b) One of them had a _____ voice.

    (c) For me cricket is the most _____ of all games.

    (d) She has invented a new kind of _____ machine.

    (e) _____ his cards on the table, he announced triumphantly: "The winner!"

3. Identify the role (noun or adjective) of each present participle:

A. (a) The Ministry of Works spent thousands of dollars on widening the Cumana road.

   (b) Antagonizing your boss will get you nowhere.

   (c) The person waving the cutlass is Benjamin.

   (d) After the fête the job of cleaning up will be yours.

   (e) They promised that the shipment would arrive the following week.

B. (a) Perched upon the table, pretending to be an ornament, was a large overfed ginger cat with a collar around its neck.
   (b) Simply climbing the stairs leaves me exhausted.
   (c) Faced with mounting opposition, the President finally resigns.
   (d) This police station serves Mt Moritz and surrounding areas.
   (e) Those pants need ironing.

C. (a) The graduating class bought a farewell present for their teacher.
   (b) After the accident I had to practise using my left hand.
   (c) Before setting out for work she feeds and dresses the baby.
   (d) The lawyer representing them was Barbara Davis.
   (e) They might be accused of meddling in the family's affairs.

Answer pp. 271-272

H2 THE CONTINUOUS TENSES

1. Formation

1.1 The continuous tenses are made up as follows:

to be + present participle.

For each of the continuous tenses a different tense of the auxiliary **to be** is used, for example:

Somebody **is using** the computer. (Present continuous)
The vendor's baby **was sleeping** peacefully in a cardboard box at her feet. (Past continuous).
That police car **has been patrolling** the area. (Present perfect continuous)

1.2 Continuous tenses are also formed with modals, for example:

We **may be fighting** our last battle.
Your aunt **should have been taking** her pills regularly.

1.3 The sentences above are in the active voice. The passive voice has a present continuous tense and a past continuous tense. For these the present and past continuous forms of the verb **to be** are placed before the past participle:

PRESENT: May's complaint **is being investigated.**
PAST: Steps **were being taken** to evict them.

2. Uses

The continuous tenses (also known as the "progressive" tenses) indicate action stretching out over a period of time, or action in progress.

2.1 The present continuous can also point to future action:

> They are taking his case to the Privy Council.

2.2 Therefore the past continuous can be used for an action or event that is "future" seen from a point in the past:

> His mother began to hope again, for they were taking his case to the Privy Council.

3. Question and negative

The question and negative forms are really the question and negative forms of the auxiliary verb **to be** followed by the main verb. Here are some examples:

QUESTION: Is somebody using the computer?
                       Are steps being taken to evict them?

NEGATIVE: We may not be fighting our last battle.
                       The rules were not being followed.

NEGATIVE QUESTION: Hasn't that police car been patrolling the area?
                       Isn't May's complaint being investigated?

4. CREOLE GRAMMAR

> *Present continuous*
>
>   TRINIDAD: We **waiting** for Jerry.
>   JAMAICA: We **a wait** pon Jerry.
>
> The Trinidadian type of Creole uses the present participle as a finite verb – the **ing** form of the verb is the present continuous.
>
> In Jamaican Creole, this tense is formed by placing **a** before the basic verb.
>
> *Past continuous*
>
>   TRINIDAD: Ambrose and he wife **was fighting**.
>   JAMAICA: Ambrose and fe him wife **did a fight**.
>
> In passive voice sentences Creole uses the same verb forms as for the active voice:
>
>   TRINIDAD: Money spending wild.
>   JAMAICA: Money a spend wild.

The Present Participle   H2

5. Pitfalls

When using the continuous tenses in English, be aware of the following pitfalls.

5.1. *Agreement*

5.1.1 Some of the continuous tenses do not require subject-verb agreement, but others do.

When the first word in a verb phrase is a modal (see E18:1.2) there is no subject-verb agreement:

My company **will be training** its own staff.
Companies **will be training** their own staff.
The child **must have been playing** with matches.
The children **must have been playing** with matches.

5.1.2 However, when the first word in the verb phrase is **to be** in the present or past tense, or **to have** in the present tense, then it must agree with the subject:

A cockroach **is crawling** up the wall.
Cockroaches **are crawling** up the wall.

The street **was being** repaired.
The streets **were being** repaired.

That police car **has been patrolling** the area.
Two police cars **have been patrolling** the area.

5.2. *Passive voice verb forms*

Remember that in English active voice verb forms cannot be used for passive voice sentences:

X *Your name is calling at this very moment.*

For the English passive voice, the continuous tenses are made up as follows:

Continuous form of **to be** + past participle.

The sentence above should therefore read:

Your name **is being called** at this very moment.

5.3 *Being v. been*

Verb forms involving the use of **being** and **been** must be handled with care, as people tend to switch the two around. This problem is discussed in H3:3.

H2 Practice

1. Make sentences from this substitution table.

I	am was have been	depending on handouts. experiencing certain difficulties.
That old man One of the players Her daughter Albert	is was has been	looking for the Passport Office. supporting the West Indies team.
The students We Some villagers You	are were have been	going to the other extreme. breaking all records. considering legal action.

See also **H3 Practice** 2.C.

2. In each of the following sentences, replace the phrase in bold type with similar phrases formed with each of the verbs given, for example:

   The highway vendors' stalls **are being removed.**

   (a) (to relocate)

   The highway vendors' stalls **are being relocated.**

A. The case **is being reviewed** by the Board.
   (a) to investigate
   (b) to take up
   (c) to reopen
   (d) to document
   (e) to monitor.

B. Players **are being selected** for the upcoming tour.
   (a) to sponsor
   (b) to choose

230

(c) to screen
   (d) to outfit
   (e) to prepare

C. I **am being transferred** to another post.
   (a) to promote
   (b) to redeploy
   (c) to move
   (d) to appoint
   (e) to demote

D. Their home **was being repainted**.
   (a) to demolish
   (b) to renovate
   (c) to refurbish
   (d) to rewire
   (e) to fumigate

E. Only two options **were being considered** by the committee.
   (a) to examine
   (b) to study
   (c) to discuss
   (d) to weigh
   (e) to entertain
   See also **H3 Practice 2.A.**

3. Convert these sentences into the passive voice (see **G5 Practice** 1):
   (a) The City Council was tearing down all the old, historic buildings.
   (b) Your child is manipulating you.
   (c) The company is not paying me overtime.
   (d) They are wasting taxpayers' money on this project.
   (e) They were not admitting children under 12.

4. Make these sentences negative, for example:

This bus is going to the airport.
> This bus is not going to the airport.
> This bus isn't going to the airport.

(a) They were having a good time.

(b) She was walking along Davies Street.

(c) Their contracts are being renewed.

(d) Nnamdi has been feeding the animals.

(e) The price of flour is being raised.

5. Convert the sentences at 4. above into questions, for example:

This bus is going to the airport.
> Is this bus going to the airport?

6. Convert the sentences at 4. above into negative questions, for example:

This bus is going to the airport.
> Isn't this bus going to the airport?

Answers pp. 272-273

H3 CONFUSING THE PARTICIPLES

1. **We have seen that both participles, past and present, can be used as adjectives.** (See G2 and H1.)

   It is important, however, that we understand the difference in meaning between the two.

   1.1 (a) Any **interested** person may write to the Ministry of Health for information on this new programme.

   (b) My neighbour is a very **interesting** person.

   What is the difference between **interested** and **interesting** in these two sentences? Each modifies the word **person**, but an "interested person" is not the same as an "interesting person".

   1.2 **Interested**, the past participle, suggests something that has been **done to** the thing that it modifies.

A person is **interested** because something has interested him or her. That person has been affected. The past participle, therefore, indicates an effect.

1.3 The present participle suggests action – the thing modified is doing something. It is active rather than acted upon.

A person who is **interesting** is a person who interests other people. That person is affecting others rather than being affected by others.

1.4 Here are some more examples:

>Please find something for these **bored** children to do.
>This is the most **boring** book I've ever read.
>
>**Disappointed** at the response of the public, the group abandoned their project.
>This has been a most **disappointing** experience.

2. **If we understand the difference in meaning between the past participle and the present participle when they are used as adjectives, we can avoid errors such as the following:**

>X *When you feel boring you can pick up a book and read.*
>X *This discussion is very interested but unfortunately I cannot stay.*

A "boring" person is a person who bores others; but if something or somebody bores you, then you are "bored".

A discussion which interests people is described as "interesting", not "interested".

These two sentences must read:

>When you feel **bored** you can pick up a book and read.
>This discussion is very **interesting**, but unfortunately I cannot stay.

3. **Being v. been**

3.1 **Being** and **been** are the two participles of **to be**.
Being is the present participle of **to be**.
Been is the past participle of **to be**.

In Creole the two words have almost the same pronunciation, and so when they occur in English verb phrases, people are not always sure which one to use. Errors such as these are often made:

>X *I have being to the United States three times.*
>X *Employees are been asked to accept a pay cut.*

These sentences should read:

> I have been to the United States three times.
> Employees are being asked to accept a pay cut.

3.2 *BEING in verb phrases*

3.2.1 The form **being** occurs in the continuous tenses (see H2) of the verb **to be**:

> This child **is being** difficult.
> You **were** not **being** honest when you made that statement.

The structure of this verb *is:* **to be** + **being**.

3.2.2 **Being** is also used in the continuous tenses of the passive voice (see G5 and H2:5.2). The verb phrase is formed as follows: **to be + being** + past participle.

> May's complaint **is being investigated**.

3.2.3 The verb **to be** (**am, is, are, was, were**) is always followed by **being**, NEVER **been**.

3.3 *BEEN in verb phrases*

3.3.1 The form **been** occurs in the perfect tenses (see G3 and G4) of the verb **to be:**

> He looks as though he **has been** through a war.
> The Town Hall **may have been** a better venue.

The structure of this verb is: **to have + been**.

3.3.2 **Been** is also used in the perfect tenses of the passive voice (see G3, G4 and G5). The verb phrase is formed as follows: **to have + been** + past participle:

> The matter **has been reported**.

3.3.3 The verb **to have** (**have, having, has, had**) is always followed by **been**, NEVER **being**.

3.3.4 **REMEMBER:**

– **am, is, are, was, were,** followed by **being**.

– **have, having, has, had** followed by **been**.

3.4 *BEING as noun and adjective*

We have seen how the present participle can be used in noun and adjective slots (H1).

Remember that the present participle of **to be** is **being**, not **been**.

Been cannot fill either a noun slot or an adjective slot. For these you need the present participle **being**, or its perfect tense form **having been** (see H1:7).

3.4.1 *Noun slots*

> **Being** impolite will get you nowhere.
> She won their trust simply by **being** patient.
> The young man apologized for **having been** negligent.

This is wrong:

> X *Been impolite will get you nowhere.*

3.4.2 *Adjective slots*

> **Being** a busy man, I have no time for trivial talk.
> **Having been** a schoolteacher, Shirley knows a thing or two about children.

This is wrong:

> X *Been a busy man, I have no time for trivial talk.*

H3 Practice

1. In each empty slot put the correct form of the verb given – past participle or present participle:
   (a) Institutions like the Small Business Development Corporation were set up to give advice to people who are _____ in becoming self-employed. (to interest)
   (b) There is nothing but _____ news on the radio. (to depress)
   (c) Lennox is seriously thinking of retiring because he is so _____ with his job. (to bore)
   (d) After the lawyer explained the fine print to me, I felt even more _____. (to confuse)
   (e) Football fans poured out of the stadium, hoarse but high in spirits, after what commentators are calling the most _____ game of the year. (to excite)

2. Make sentences from these substitution tables.

The Knots In English

A.

I	am was	being	given another opportunity.
You June and Wendell The girls	are were		urged to claim compensation. blamed for everything. kept in the dark. described as unreliable.
That young man My colleague Anne-Marie	is was		deported from this country. taken for a ride.

B.

I You June and Wendell The girls	have	been	given another opportunity. urged to claim compensation. blamed for everything. kept in the dark.
That young man My colleague Anne-Marie	has		described as unreliable. deported from this country. taken for a ride.

C.

I They The Alleynes Some people	have	been	taking things too seriously. enjoying the good life. watching the world go by. hoping for a miracle.
Sunil Your friend Mr Lee Lum She	has		going to a keep-fit class. cooking without salt. toying with the idea.

3. In each of the following sentences, replace the phrase in bold type with similar phrases formed with each of the verbs given, for example:

> He does not remember **being shot**.
> (a) (to tell)
> He does not remember **being told**.

A. We certainly did not enjoy **being evicted**.
   (a) to attack
   (b) to ridicule
   (c) to chase
   (d) to victimize
   (e) to fleece

B. Returning travellers spoke of **having been harassed** by Immigration officers.
   (a) to interrogate
   (b) to detain
   (c) to welcome
   (d) to intimidate
   (e) to caution

C. Mr Hewitt arrived on the scene just as the men **were being dismissed**.
   (a) to pay
   (b) to brief
   (c) to warn
   (d) to recruit
   (d) to photograph

D. They were commended for not **having been swayed** by their peers.
   (a) to influence
   (b) to subvert
   (c) to discourage
   (d) to dissuade
   (e) to distract

E. One year after **being elected**, he packed his bags and migrated to the USA.
   (a) to release
   (b) to convict
   (c) to hire
   (d) to appoint
   (e) to indict

4. In each empty slot put the correct form of the verb **to be** – **been** or **being**:
   (a) The child would avoid _____ punished by adhering to rules.
   (b) Having _____ selected to represent her country, she had to undergo a rigorous training programme.
   (c) Media advertisement has not only _____ beneficial to businesses but it has also benefitted customers.
   (d) Not _____ able to complete college has been a setback.
   (e) Customers were _____ given the runaround.

5. Correct the wrong participles in the following sentences:
   (a) *Having this kind of job makes me feel more frustrating.*
   (b) *I saw a garbage bin overflowed with such things as cans, bottles and decaying food.*
   (c) *Been Minister of Trade and Tourism he is always overburdened with work.*
   (d) *The villagers are suffering from a variety of diseases resulted from pollution.*
   (e) *The protesting women marched around the Savannah with lighting candles in their hands.*

Answers p. 273

ANSWERS

A1 NOUNS

2. A. (a) police, suspects
   (b) newspapers, names
   (c) court, Wednesday
   (d) lawyer, Barbara Davis
   (e) case, date, February

2. B. (a) Trevor, Naima, race, year
   (b) marathon, event
   (c) months, day
   (d) distance
   (e) Trevor, Naima, prize, experience

2. C. (a) panside, anniversary, week
   (b) name, band, Panthers
   (c) members, LaGrange, communities
   (d) celebration, savannah
   (e) food, drinks, games, music

A2 PRONOUNS

1. (a) She (b) them (c) him (d) himself (e) her

2. *These are the pronouns in each sentence:*
   A. (a) we (b) she (c) me, that (d) somebody (e) they
   B. (a) everything (b) us (c) yours (d) these (e) her
   C. (a) it (b) herself (c) them (d) him (e) that
   D. (a) their (b) my (c) his (d) our (e) its

A3 ADJECTIVES

1. *Words modified:*
   A. (a) village (b) children (c) problem (d) courthouse (e) day
   B. (a) she (b) essay (c) road, we (d) it (e) you

C. (a) people (b) it (c) man (d) meeting (e) myself
D. (a) town (b) play (c) farmer (d) people (e) questions

Adjectives:	Words modified:
2. A. (a) small	garden
(b) thick	bush
(c) hard, stony	ground
(d) difficult	task
young, energetic, full	they
(e) large,	garden
productive	it

Adjectives:	Words modified:
B. (a) bitter	argument
(b) full	sink
dirty	dishes
(c) important	something
(d) lazy	Neil
dirty	dishes
(e) loud	argument
angry	voice
empty	sink

A4 VERBS

1. A. (a) to see   B. (a) to decide
   (b) to eat   (b) to spin
   (c) to speak   (c) to lose
   (d) to catch   (d) to approach
   (e) to announce   (e) to wear

   C. (a) to succeed   D (a) to choose
   (b) to contain   (b) to steal
   (c) to concentrate   (c) to sink
   (d) to describe   (d) to shake
   (e) to attempt   (e) to fly

Answers

2. A. (a) stopped (b) owe (c) operates (d) gave (e) is

   B. (a) is holding (b) did reach (c) have submitted (d) would believe (e) can accommodate

   C. (a) are being terminated
      (b) will have gone
      (c) has been sent
      (d) may be adopted
      (e) should have revealed

3. A1-1.

   A. (a) was damaged
      (b) voted
      (c) was going; appeared
      (d) reported; had resigned
      (e) will be held

   B. (a) saw
      (b) have closed
      (c) found
      (d) lacks
      (e) were throwing

   C. (a) are taken; should be implemented
      (b) are going to find
      (c) plies; is
      (d) received
      (e) was announced

   D. (a) is (b) were (c) was (d) stands (e) are

A1-2.
   A. (a) arrested (b) were allowed (c) appeared (d) was (e) was adjourned
   B. (a) entered (b) is (c) trained (d) became; were (e) won; enjoyed
   C. (a) celebrates (b) is (c) live (d) will be held (e) will be

A5 ADVERBS

Adverbs:	Words modified:
A. (a) more	carefully
carefully	must write
(b) almost	illegible
(c) forward	lean
backwards	lean
(d) sometimes	chase
crazily	chase
(e) always	think
B. (a) regularly	visit
(b) really	is
(c) perfectly	happy
(d) quite	strict
never	spoils
(e) rarely	misbehave
C. (a) yesterday	was held
(b) afterwards	cleaned
(c) swiftly	worked
efficiently	worked
(d) upstairs	worked
downstairs	worked
(e) practically	new

Answers

A6 PREPOSITIONS

2.

	Prepositions:	Nouns governed:	Prepositional phrases:
A.	(a) to	hall	to the union hall
	(b) for	directions	for directions
	(c) down	Grant Street	down Grant Street
	(d) at	light	at the traffic light
	(e) on	right	on their right
B.	(a) in	house	in his house
	(b) on	couch	on the couch
	(c) under	table	under the dining-room table
	into	ball	into a ball
	next to	mother	next to its mother
	(d) behind	sideboard	behind the sideboard
	(e) upon	centre-table	upon the centre-table
	with	collar	with a collar
	around	neck	around its neck
C.	(a) into	supermarket	into the supermarket
	with	child	with a small child
	(b) by	experience	by bitter experience
	(c) into	Food Fair	into Food Fair
	(d) onto	counters	onto counters
	off	shelves	off shelves
	around	legs	around the legs
	of	customers	of customers
	(e) in	future	in future
	at	home	at home
	to	supermarket	to the supermarket

3. A1-1. C. (a) by, without (b) in (c) to, of (d) for (e) after, of

4. A2-2. C. (a) for (b) to (c) with (d) in (e) of

243

A7 CONJUNCTIONS

1. when (1.1); but (1.6); and (1.7); and (1.11).

2. (a) unless (b) and (c) if (d) and (e) because

3. A. (a) so (b) or (c) but (d) but (e) and

   B. (a) until (b) because (c) why (d) when (e) since

B2 THE SUBJECT

	Subjects:	Verbs:
A.	(a) we	assembled
	(b) Grace	is talking
	(c) Aruna	seemed
	(d) all	live
	(e) chickens	are roaming
B.	(a) it	was
	they	were
	(b) argument	got
	Tantie	shouted
	sink	was
	(c) work	stopped
	(d) going	is
	(e) everyone	will have gone
C.	(a) she	stood
	(b) it	rains
	you	can't drive
	(c) they	misbehave
	(d) group	worked
	(e) school	looks

Answers

B3 THE OBJECT

	Subjects:	Verbs:	Objects:
A.	(a) police	arrested	suspects
	(b) they	appeared	
	(c) Trevor and Naima	entered	race
	(d) they	trained	
	(e) panside	celebrates	anniversary
B.	(a) Ma Charlotte	walked	
	(b) that	embarrassed	him
	(c) they	cut	bush
	(d) they	forked	ground
	(e) you	must write	
C.	(a) they	visit	grandmother
	(b) Sylvie	crept	
	(c) organizers	cleaned	place
	(d) Mr Richards	had	cats
	(e) she	took	cousin

B4 THE INDIRECT OBJECT

	Direct objects:	Indirect objects:
A.	(a) house	grandparents
	(b) drink	her
	(c) manners	children
	(d) moment	me
	(e) breakfast	passengers
B.	(a) warrant	Craig
	(b) accommodation	students
	(c) place	school
	(d) secrets	Laila
	(e) sandwiches	themselves

B5 THE COMPLEMENT

1.
	Subjects:	Verbs:	Complements:
A.	(a) Sylvie	felt	weak
	(c) calypso	sounds	good
	(d) Sarah	was	child
B.	(b) houses	had become	heaps
	(c) job	will be	yours
	(d) dog	looks	fierce
C.	(a) fish	has gone	bad
	(b) demolition	is becoming	issue
	(c) son	has turned	Catholic
	(e) question	is	why did this happen

2.
Objects:	Object complements:
(a) this	breach
(b) place	clean
(c) her	Mother
(d) contract	null and void
(e) me	dead

B6 PHRASES AND CLAUSES

1. A. (a) subordinate clause (b) phrase (c) sentence (d) sentence (e) subordinate clause
   B. (a) phrase (b) subordinate clause (c) phrase (d) sentence (e) sentence
   C. (a) sentence (b) subordinate clause (c) subordinate clause (d) phrase (e) sentence

2. A. (a) it is essential
      (b) she would have walked
      (c) Professor Chung began his lecture
      (d) the garden was not large
         it was productive
      (e) they call themselves twins

Answers

B. (a) we will build our grandparents a new house
   (b) they became very fit
       both were able to run the whole distance
   (c) nothing will be done
   (d) it rushes
   (e) traffic was diverted

3. A. If you write illegibly in an exam then you have failed before you even start. The examiners are not going to waste time trying to decipher what you have written when they might have hundreds of other papers to mark. Bad handwriting is bad manners. It shows a lack of consideration for those who have to read what you write.

   B. About three years ago a new law was passed making it an offence to litter streets and other public places. People ignored it at first and continued to treat the whole country as one large dustbin. Driving along the highways they threw beer bottles and cigarette boxes out of cars. In the towns and villages streets were still strewn with every kind of rubbish casually dropped by pedestrians or piled on the pavement by businesspeople. A river was a place where you could throw anything from a dead dog to a derelict motor car. After about a week the police actually started to prosecute people for littering. The offenders were quite indignant. They thought it was perfectly in order to fling away things that they didn't need any longer. It was a clear case of the government violating people's human rights. The courts slapped some heavy fines on those found guilty of littering and people soon began to appreciate the human right of all citizens to live in a clean environment.

C1 SINGULAR AND PLURAL

	Singular nouns	*Plural nouns*
A.	(a) foot, hill	
	(b)	days
	(c) photographer, picture	records
	(d) place	chickens
	(e) request	locks
B.	(a) sink	dishes
	(b) response, pressure opinion, report	

	Singular nouns	*Plural nouns*
	c) child	counters, things, shelves, legs, customers
	(d) centre-table, ornament cat, collar, neck	
	(e) food, music	drinks, games
C.	(a) house	grandparents
	(b) dog, vehicle, road	
	(c) drink, brandy	
	(d) calypso	
	(e) demolition, issue	houses

C2 DIFFERENT WAYS OF ADDING S
    (a) decoys, matches, possibilities, leaves, beaches
    (b) stitches, dictionaries, chiefs, dishes, parties
    (c) highways, wharves, companies, faxes, families
    (d) holidays, losses, assemblies, scarves, classes
    (e) cliffs, patches, attorneys, wolves, copies

C3 OTHER PLURAL FORMS
    (a) campuses, synopses, phenomenon, focuses/foci, goose
    (b) memoranda, person, bases, cactuses/cacti, formula
    (c) stadiums/stadia, analysis, metamorphoses, curriculum, choruses
    (d) larva, nucleuses/nuclei, syllabuses/syllabi, symposium, appendices
    (e) louse, hypotheses, electrons, fisherman, antennae.

C4 PLURAL MARKERS: CREOLE V. ENGLISH
1.   (a) scholarships (b) students (c) advertisements (d) friends (e) restaurants
3.   (a) People scattered in all directions when the bomb went off.
    (b) There are two distinct seasons in this country.
    (c) These new techniques have raised many moral and ethical questions.
    (d) Most young adults have problems of one kind or another.
    (e) Quite a few of these songs promote violence.

Answers

C5 COUNTABLE AND UNCOUNTABLE NOUNS

1. **Countable nouns**: streets, city, mosquitoes, earthquake, cigarettes, highway, pictures, chair, months, villages, students, cow

   Uncountable nouns: milk, oxygen, dirt, smoke, rubbish, laziness, clay, justice, steel, cocoa, labour, intelligence

2. **Countable nouns**: house, eyes, building, step, sight, hurricane, roofs, neighbours', houses, pieces, shapes, trees, roots, houses, heaps, people, town, place

   Uncountable nouns: damage, destruction, safety, horror, metal, timber

3. chicken: (a) uncountable (d) plural countable
   (i) singular countable

   experience: (b) uncountable (e) singular countable (j) plural countable

   crime: (c) plural countable (k) singular countable (o) uncountable

   oil: (f) singular countable (h) uncountable (m) plural countable

   beer: (g) uncountable (i) singular countable (n) plural countable

C6 USE OF DETERMINERS

1.

DETERMINER	NOUN	DESCRIPTION OF NOUN
A. (a) some	dogs	plural countable
	thunder	uncountable
(b) a	ghost	singular countable
(c)	people	plural countable
	marijuana	uncountable
that	forest	singular countable
(d) a	restaurant	singular countable
(e) a	bulldozer	singular countable
the	hill	singular countable
B. (a) an	aeroplane	singular countable
the	islands	plural countable
(b) this	month	singular countable
	eggs	plural countable

249

DETERMINER	NOUN	DESCRIPTION OF NOUN
(c) that	information	uncountable
a	book	singular countable
(d)	books	plural countable
	knowledge	uncountable
	enjoyment	uncountable
(e) the	time	singular countable
C. (a) your	raincoat	singular countable
(b)	dots	plural countable
his	eyes	plural countable
(c) that	firm	singular countable
	cars	plural countable
(d) the	love	uncountable
	money	uncountable
the	root	singular countable
	evil	uncountable
(e) an	election	singular countable

2. A. (a) effects/a lasting effect (b) trade unions (c) such a term (d) accidents (e) jobs

B. (a) organizations (b) situations (c) developments (d) a women's movement/women's movements (e) such an institution/such institutions

C. (a) The infant mortality rate (b) the number of accidents (c) a/the family unit (d) the cess (e) such students; scholarships; scholarships

C7 ARTICLES: WHEN TO USE AN

A. (a) an (b) a (c) an (d) an (e) a

B. (a) a (b) an (c) an (d) a (e) a

C. (a) a (b) an (c) an (d) a (e) an

… Answers

C8 NOUNS WITH QUANTITY EXPRESSIONS

2. fun, pencils, questions, work, concrete, shoes, cocoa, meat, problems, appointments, hands, asphalt, towns, teachers, names, rum, letters, smoke, buttons, leather

3. **too much** fun, work, concrete, cocoa, meat, asphalt, rum smoke, leather

   too many pencils, questions, shoes, problems, appointments, hands, towns, teachers, names, letters, buttons

5. (a) An alarming number of young people
   (b) Much of our vegetation
   (c) as many people
   (d) a limited number of vendors
   (e) much of the equipment

6. (a) Most Caribbean music
   (b) most of their day
   (c) for most of the year
   (d) most praedial larceny
   (e) for most of the time

C9 ONE OF…

4. (a) reasons (b) drugs (c) dogs (d) days (e) disadvantages

C10 NOUNS ENDING WITH A SOUND LIKE S

1.
tests	disguises	phrases	conveniences
places	wrists	guests	vests
quizzes	addresses	traces	classes
circumstances	posts	prizes	artists
lists	discs	breasts	ghosts
exercises	pianists	appliances	nurses
glasses	losses	tasks	faces

2. (a) businesses (b) consequences (c) scientists (d) places (e) desks

C11 SOME PROBLEM NOUNS

A. (a) certain pieces of baggage
   (b) a very unique piece of sporting equipment

(c) garbage
(d) He is painting tropical scenery.
   He is painting a tropical scene.
(e) the furniture

B. (a) The youngster was wearing very expensive sneakers.
   The youngster was wearing a very expensive pair of sneakers.
(b) one pair of scissors
(c) wearing blue pants
(d) a pair of glasses
(e) one single mouse

D1 FORMING THE POSSESSIVE

1. (a) lawyer's - singular
      client's - singular
   (b) postmen's - plural
   (c) years' - plural
      teachers' - plural
   (d) party's - singular
   (e) school's - singular

2. A. (a) a baby's   (b) Asha's
      (c) the artist's   (d) Garvin's
      (e) Mr Inniss'/Mr Inniss's

   B. (a) most people's   (b) Rastafarians'
      (c) some teachers'   (d) the men's
      (e) these ladies'

3. (a) a family's food bills
   a person's food bills
   a household's food bills
   (b) the actress'/actress's picture
   the fugitive's picture
   the suspect's picture
   (c) some members' car tyres
   some customers' car tyres
   some lecturers' car tyres

Answers

(d) the board's reaction
Chris'/Chris's reaction
my colleague's reaction
(e) children's pastimes
pensioners' pastimes
consumers' pastimes

D2 FORMING THE POSSESSIVE WITH OF

A. (a) This film shows how the body of the man who got hit reacted to the blow.
(b) the resources of this universe
(c) The name of the band's sponsor was announced
(d) The income of television networks
(e) This can cause a further breakdown of parent-child relations.

B. (a) the name of the person heading the committee
(b) the presence of terminally ill patients in our society
(c) The classrooms of public schools
(d) The major application of fibre optics
(e) the growth of the tourist industry

C. (a) the role of the African National Congress in dismantling apartheid
(b) the all-round education of the Natural Science student
(c) The cosmopolitan character of Trinidad and Tobago's population
(d) The organization of the research paper
(e) the volume of their radios

D3 THE POSSESSIVE: COMMON ERRORS

1. (a) this student's work (b) Caribbean's (c) farmers' (d) the builder's tools (e) society's
(f) neighbours' (g) women's (h) stoves (i) destroys

2. A. (a) receptionist's (b) viewers' (c) human being's (d) challenges (e) puppies'
B. (a) nation's (b) dogs' (c) the sun's rays (d) children's (e) motorists
C. (a) the child's academic grades (b) people's (c) works (d) hostages' (e) bird's

D4 POSSESSIVE NOUNS V. ADJECTIVAL NOUNS

   A. (a) Salvation (b) cricket (c) telephone (d) insurance (e) Trinidad, tourist

   B. (a) dog (b) organ (c) election (d) Agriculture, field (e) bullet

   C. (a) union (b) traffic (c) calypso (d) cheese (e) television

2. (a) apple vendors (b) short story writer (c) louvre windows (d) poor road conditions (e) drug prevention

E1 FORMING THE PRESENT SIMPLE TENSE

A.	(a) to succeed	succeed	succeeds
	(b) to happen	happen	happens
	(c) to steal	steal	steals
	(d) to describe	describe	describes
	(e) to teach	teach	teaches
B.	(a) to increase	increase	increases
	(b) to take	take	takes
	(c) to fight	fight	fights
	(d) to fly	fly	flies
	(e) to stain	stain	stains
C.	(a) to write	write	writes
	(b) to construct	construct	constructs
	(c) to belong	belong	belongs
	(d) to sit	sit	sits
	(e) to spin	spin	spins

2. A. (a) celebrates (b) live (c) controls (d) has (e) owe
   B. (a) operates (b) misbehave (c) looks (d) sleep (e) chairs
   C. (a) remains (b) sounds (c) use (d) hears, rushes (e) prefer

Answers

E2 USES OF THE PRESENT SIMPLE TENSE

A. (a) live (b) finish (c) rings (d) sing (e) takes

B. (a) find (b) takes (c) learn (d) starts (e) leave

C. (a) invades (b) puts (c) find, flag (d) turns, gives (e) join, falls, come

D. (a) like (b) knows (c) wishes (d) prefer (e) want

E. (a) takes (b) steps, lays (c) moves, sticks (d) roll (e) strikes

Functions:

A. Habitual action

B. Future action

C. Past action dramatized

D. Mental action in the present

E. Live reporting

E3 WHEN TO PUT THE *S*

SUBJECTS USED WITH BARE VERB	SUBJECTS USED WITH VERB + S ENDING
nurses	earth
babies	she
exams	Minister
you	car
they	President
I	he
children	she
	Peterson
	cortège

E4 THE PRESENT TENSE: CREOLE INFLUENCE

1 A. (a) Some drivers try (b) He has (d) Our teacher gives

   B. (b) drugs do (d) The children have (e) the cisterns and gutters overflow

2. 2.1 stands, believes
    2.2 contribute, enable

3. (a) Every morning when I get up, I brush my teeth. Then I bathe. Next I put on my clothes and I eat breakfast. Then my mother gives me money for busfare. My friend comes to meet me and we go to the bus stop together.

   (b) A secretary types letters for her boss. She answers the phone. A secretary files documents. She makes appointments for her boss. The boss dictates letters to her and she writes them down in shorthand.

E5 THE VERB TO BE

2. (a) are (b) is (c) are (d) is (e) am

4. A. (a) The effects are (d) vehicles are (e) I, for example, am
   B. (c) Your role is (d) The small space and lack of exercise are

E6 IDENTIFYING THE HEAD WORD

1. A. (a) report (b) adopting (c) temperature (d) cars (e) children
   B. (a) lawyer (b) review (c) roofs d) attempts (e) competition
   C. (a) situation (b) facilities (c) cat (d) building (e) signs
   D. (a) cousin (b) women (c) governments (d) daughter (e) repainting
   E. (a) safety (b) members (c) going (d) villages (e) person

2. A. (a) sleep (b) offers (c) pollutes (d) welcomes (e) is
   B. (a) collects (b) falls (c) invites (d) lack (e) remains
   C. (a) organizes (b) cause (c) become (d) offers (e) damages

3. A. (b) wear (c) changes (d) is
   B. (d) have (e) turn
   C. (a) are (b) belong (d) get

4. (a) The cost of secondary school texts is
   (b) Some raucous men fixing the road outside our house start
   (c) A full and detailed report sent to the directors of the firm contains
   (d) Smoking so many cigarettes has

E7 PRESENT TENSE VERBS IN JOINED SENTENCES

1. A. (a) Henry cleans... and does (b) the neighbours clean... and do (c) she cleans... and does
   (d) the eldest child cleans... and does (e) working women clean... and do

Answers

B. (a) The adults in my home hate... but tolerate (b) Our teacher hates... but tolerates (c) Mr Oliver and his wife hate... but tolerate (d) This child hates... but tolerates (e) Certain people hate... but tolerate

C. (a) my grandmother wakes up... and attends (b) Rose and her children wake up... and attend (c) that hypocrite wakes up... and attends (d) the children wake up... and attend (e) the whole village wakes up... and attends

D. (a) The fish vendors arrive... set out their stock... and await
   (b) The man with the pumpkins arrives... sets out his stock... and awaits...
   (c) People selling in the Tunapuna market arrive... set out their stock... and await
   (d) George and his partner arrive... set out their stock... and await
   (e) You arrive... set out your stock... and await

E. (a) you feed and dress... make up... manage
   (b) one feeds and dresses... makes up... manages
   (c) Kathleen feeds and dresses... makes up... manages
   (d) these women feed and dress... make up... manage
   (e) my aunt feeds and dresses... makes up... manages

2. A. (a) disconnects (b) call (c) has (d) lacks (e) are
   B. (a) enters (b) feels (c) makes (d) wishes (e) becomes

E8 VERB BEFORE SUBJECT

1. A. (a) is (b) comes (c) run (d) grows (e) are
   B. (a) goes (b) are (c) comes (d) is (e) lie

E9 THERE IS/ARE

2. (a) there are (b) There are (c) there is (d) there are (e) There is

3. (a) continue (b) remains (c) exist (d) appears (e) comes

E10 RELATIVE PRONOUN AS SUBJECT

1. A. (a) and (c) to be joined to:

who have nothing to lose
who live in the housing settlement
who work the hardest
who donate blood regularly
who fear the police
(b), (d) and (e) to be joined to the rest

B. (b), (d) and (e) to be joined to:

which create conflict
which are not relevant to the discussion
which offend certain groups
which have no basis
which make no sense
(a) and (c) to be joined to the rest

C. (a), (d) and (e) to be joined to:

that seems feasible
that solves the problems identified
that takes all these issues into consideration
that has the potential to succeed
that makes more sense than previous ones of its kind

2. (a) affect (b) who are interested (d) runs

E11 SUBJECTS WITH QUANTITY EXPRESSIONS

1. A. (a) are (b) is (c) is (d) are (e) are
   B. (a) is (b) is (c) are (d) are (e) is

2. A. (a) has (b) have (c) have (d) has (e) has
   B. (a) receives (b) receive (c) receive (d) receive (e) receives
   C. (a) fits (b) fit (c) fits (d) fits (e) fit
   D. (a) belong (b) belongs (c) belongs (d) belong (e) belongs
   E. (a) knows (b) know (c) knows (d) know (e) knows

E12 VERBS ENGING WITH A SOUND LIKE S

(a) wastes (b) exist (c) suggests (d) addresses (e) force

Answers

E13 UNCHANGEABLE NOUN AS SUBJECT

2. (a) confuses (b) work (c) make (d) cut (e) is

E14 QUESTION FORM OF THE PRESENT SIMPLE TENSE

2A. (a) Do you agree with everything he says?
   (b) Does Ms Ramdeen chair the general meeting?
   (c) Do the candidates understand what is required of them?
   (d) Does she want one of those?
   (e) Do Michael and his sister sing in the choir?

B. (a) Does the fish-processing company employ people living in the area?
   (b) Do female members participate equally at all levels of the organization?
   (c) Do social workers visit the home on a regular basis?
   (d) Does each student choose a different topic?
   (e) Do soap operas appeal to all kinds of people?

C. (a) Does the temperature in this room suit everybody?
   (b) Do rank-and-file members of the party support this decision?
   (c) Do public health care facilities stay open on weekends?
   (d) Does the lawyer representing them know where they are?
   (e) Does the person driving the car have a driver's permit?

E15 NEGATIVE FORM OF THE PRESENT SIMPLE TENSE

2. A. (a) You do not agree... /You don't agree...
   (b) Ms Ramdeen does not chair.../Ms Ramdeen doesn't chair...
   (c) The candidates do not understand.../The candidates don't understand...
   (d) She does not want.../She doesn't want...
   (e) Michael and his sister do not sing.../Michael and his sister don't sing...

B. (a) The temperature... does not suit.../The temperature... doesn't suit...
   (b) members of the party do not support.../ ... members of the party don't support...
   (c) facilities do not stay open.../facilities don't stay open...
   (d) The lawyer... does not know.../The lawyer... doesn't know...
   (e) The person... does not have.. ./The person... doesn't have...

3. A. (a) do not make/don't make
   (b) does not leave/doesn't leave
   (c) do not abuse/don't abuse
   (d) do not convince/don't convince
   (e) does not have/doesn't have

   B. (a) do not give/don't give
   (b) does not shed/doesn't shed
   (c) does not extend/doesn't extend
   (d) do not intend/don't intend
   (e) does not accept/doesn't accept

E16 DOUBLE NEGATIVES

1. A. (a) The sugar estate does not/doesn't pay its workers a/any bonus
       The sugar estate pays its workers no bonus
   (b) These young people do not have/don't have (any) plans
       These young people have no plans
   (c) Mr Henry does not/doesn't need (any) help
       Mr Henry needs no help
   (d) Health centres do not/don't handle (any) major ailments
       Health centres handle no major ailments.
   (e) Government does not/doesn't provide (any) support
       Government provides no support

   B. (a) These figures do not/don't give us any indication
       These figures give us no indication
   (b) Paula does not/doesn't know anybody in Port-of-Spain.
       Paula knows nobody in Port-of-Spain.
   (c) My brothers do not/don't do any of the housework.
       My brothers do none of the housework.
   (d) Residents... do not/don't contribute anything towards
       Residents... contribute nothing towards

Answers

    (e) Brian does not/doesn't keep any for himself.

        Brian keeps none for himself.

2.   (a) No bus passes here.

    (b) The people behind the desk don't care about anybody.

    (c) That company never observes any safety precautions.

    (d) Nobody named "Oliver" lives at this address.

    (e) When you get money you hardly put aside any.

E17 PRESENT SIMPLE TENSE: NEGATIVE QUESTIONS

2. A. (a) Don't all of our members live...?

    (b) Doesn't Mr Barnes control...?

    (c) Don't government ministries owe...?

    (d) Doesn't Sylvester operate...?

    (e) Doesn't Ms Ramdeen chair...?

  B. (a) Doesn't his latest calypso sound...?

    (b) Don't they use...?

    (c) Doesn't she work...?

    (d) Don't exams begin...?

    (e) Don't you agree...?

  C. (a) Don't Michael and his sister sing...?

    (b) Don't the candidates understand...?

    (c) Doesn't the person driving the car have...?

    (d) Don't social workers visit...?

    (e) Doesn't the fish processing company employ...?

E18 WHERE NOT TO PUT THE S

1. (a) Romain does not forget

    (b) Why must one person hold...?

    (c) She does not return

    (d) It may seem

    (e) He does not have

2. (a) can boast (b) must turn (c) may participate (d) can choose (e) may sit

3. (a) Can the Parent-Teachers' Association boast...?
   (b) Must he turn off...?
   (c) May female members participate...?
   (d) Can each student choose...?
   (e) May first-formers sit...?

4. (a) cannot boast (b) must not turn off (c) may not participate (d) cannot choose (e) may not sit

10. (a) enroll (b) be free (c) focus (d) be an option (e) study

E20 THE VERB *TO BE*: NEGATIVE FORM

2. (a) is not/isn't (b) are not/aren't (c) is not/isn't (d) are not/aren't (e) are not/aren't

3. (a) The boy is not a bandit.
   The boy is no bandit.
   The boy is not any bandit.
   (b) I am nobody's slave.
   I am not anybody's slave.
   (c) That isn't any way to treat your child.
   That's no way to treat your child.
   (d) You aren't any angel yourself.
   You're no any angel yourself.
   (e) These young thugs are not afraid of anything.
   These young thugs are afraid of nothing.

E21 THE VERB *TO BE*: NEGATIVE QUESTIONS

2. A. (a) Isn't access to information a...?
   Is access to information not a...?
   (b) Aren't we under a...?
   Are we not under a...?
   (c) Aren't I eligible...?
   Am I not eligible...?

(d) Isn't that the whole...?
   Is that not the whole...?
(e) Aren't toy guns on...?
   Are toy guns not on...?

B. (a) Isn't the county of St David under...?
   Is the county of St David not under...?
(b) Aren't rape and murder serious...?
   Are rape and murder not serious...?
(c) Aren't you Miss Adeline's...?
   Are you not Miss Adeline's...?
(d) Isn't Gregory a member...?
   Is Gregory not a member...?
(e) Isn't divestment pretty much...?
   Is divestment not pretty much...?

C. (a) Aren't these people willing...?
   Are these people not willing...?
(b) Isn't this a...?
   Is this not a...?
(c) Aren't they on...?
   Are they not on...?
(d) Isn't embezzlement punishable...?
   Is embezzlement not punishable...?
(e) Aren't elections due...?
   Are elections not due...?

F1 FORMING THE PAST SIMPLE TENSE

1. A. (a) cleaned (b) appeared (c) entered (d) stopped (e) worked
   B. (a) became (b) found (c) began (d) gave (e) took
   C. (a) left (b) crept (c) bought (d) felt (e) spent

2. A. (a) supplied (b) owed (c) supported (d) paid (e) went
   B. (a) controlled (b) stayed (c) slept (d) sang (e) built
   C. (a) looked (b) called (c) chaired (d) were (e) knew

F2 VERBS WHICH DO NOT CHANGE

1. (a) read (b) cut (c) beat (d) cost (e) broadcast

2. (a) increased, burst, had (b) got, shut, let (c) spread, began (d) cost, had (e) kept, split

F3 PAST TENSE VERBS IN JOINED SENTENCES

1. A. (a) stole (b) borrowed (c) picked up (d) got (e) selected
   B. (a) assured (b) told (c) notified (d) reminded (e) advised
   C. (a) reprimanded (b) praised (c) upbraided (d) commended (e) rewarded
   D. (a) offloaded (b) deposited (c) left (d) threw (e) spread
   E. (a) clapped (b) protested (c) argued (d) applauded (e) chanted

2. (a) travelled (b) built (c) raided (d) as time went by (e) fixed, called

F4 VERBS ENDING WITH A SOUND LIKE D

1. A. (a) adopted (b) needed (c) rejected (d) attracted (e) avoided
   B. (a) resulted (b) stood (c) disconnected (d) limited (e) ended

2. (a) attended (b) assisted (c) ended (d) added (e) fought

F5 QUESTION FORM OF THE PAST SIMPLE TENSE

2. A. (a) Did Allyson get...?
      (b) Did the organizers clean...?
      (c) Did Trevor and Naima enter...?
      (d) Did the school give...?
      (e) Did they appear...?

   B. (a) Did he tell them...?
      (b) Did they go...?
      (c) Did Ma Charlotte walk...?
      (d) Did the children find...?
      (e) Did he put...?

Answers

F6 NEGATIVE FORM OF THE PAST SIMPLE TENSE

1. A. (a) Allyson did not/didn't get
    (b) The organizers did not/didn't clean
    (c) Trevor and Naima did not/didn't enter
    (d) The school did not/didn't give
    (e) They did not/didn't appear

   B. (a) He did not/didn't tell
    (b) They did not/didn't go
    (c) Ma Charlotte did not/didn't walk
    (d) The children did not/didn't find
    (e) He did not/didn't put

2. (a) I didn't see a man/any man
    (b) did not have
    (c) didn't
    (d) didn't find any
    (e) didn't eat anything

F7 WHEN NOT TO USE PAST TENSE FORM

5. A. (a) to sign (b) strike (c) change (d) boil (e) agree
   B. (a) assess (b) alarm (c) admire (d) quote (e) say

F8 THE VERB *TO BE*: PAST SIMPLE TENSE

2. (a) was (b) were (c) were (d) was (e) were

3. A. (a) Why were the two boys...?
    (b) Why were you...?
    (c) Why was Miriam's watch...?
    (d) Why were certain people...?
    (e) Why was nobody...?

   B. (a) When was Roanna...?
    (b) When was Maurice Bishop...?

(c) When were you...?

(d) When was this gentleman...?

(e) When were government ministers...?

4. (a) was not/wasn't

   (b) were not/weren't

   (c) were not/weren't

   (d) was not/wasn't

   (e) were not/weren't

5. (a) Wasn't Miriam's watch...?

   (b) Weren't certain people...?

   (c) Weren't you...?

   (d) Wasn't this gentleman...?

   (e) Weren't government ministers...?

6. (a) there was a long delay

   (c) most of the people... were

   (d) one of the more strict school rules was

F10 COULD AND WOULD

1. (a) Rose thought it would take too long.

   (b) They estimated that they could be

   (c) You could not register unless you paid

   (d) He said that there wouldn't be

   (e) The suspect agreed to give himself up if the authorities would guarantee

2. (a) In such an environment one can do as one pleases.

   (b) Nobody can understand what he means.

   (c) We have no reason to doubt that the funds will be available.

   (d) That child can turn perfect cartwheels.

   (e) I have a feeling that it won't work.

3. A. (a) I will tell you

   (b) they could study

Answers

   (c) workers would be
   (d) service will be held
   (e) the only people who can tell

  B. (a) they would go
   (b) the Caribbean will not develop
   (c) an attack... could come
   (d) The difficult situation... will improve
   (e) who could make

5. (a) would (b) will/can (c) would (d) would/could (e) will/can

7. (a) could have taken
    (b) could see
    (c) would have called
    (d) would have passed
    (e) would be

8. (a) Could you put the food in the fridge.
    (b) Would you like to take some of the flowers with you?
    (c) Would you please turn down that radio.
    (d) Could you file these letters before you go.
    (e) Would you like to taste our rum punch?

10. (a) he tells you
    (b) only candidates... qualify to do
    (c) we eat lunch
    (d) one needs fewer calories
    (e) expenses are high

G1 IDENTIFYING THE PAST PARTICIPLE

1. (a) enclosed
    (b) built
    (c) parked
    (d) advanced
    (e) chosen

267

2. (a) seen; have seen
   (b) ended; had ended
   (c) taken; would have taken
   (d) made; will have made
   (e) risen; has risen

3. (a) felt; it is felt
   (b) undertaken; will be undertaken
   (c) organized; was organized
   (d) offered; were offered
   (e) done; can be done

G2 THE PAST PARTICIPLE AS ADJECTIVE

1. A. (a) ransacked (b) demolished (c) painted (d) fenced (e) decorated
   B. (a) pursued (b) implemented (c) outlined (d) adopted (e) proposed
   C. (a) irritated (b) depressed (c) pleased (d) occupied (d) discouraged
   D. (a) disconnected (b) regularized (c) restored (d) stabilized (e) turned on.
   E. (a) impressed (b) annoyed (c) elated (d) disappointed (f) frustrated.

2. A. (a) gained (b) experienced (c) wedge-shaped (d) puzzled (d) disciplined
   B. (a) increased (b) frizzled (c) old-fashioned (d) required (e) involved
   C. (a) biased (b) surprised (c) accustomed (d) concerned (e) pleased.

3. A. (a) knowledge (b) politician (c) head (d) you (e) teacher
   B. (a) inflow (b) fowl (c) practice (d) skills (e) risks
   C. (a) letters (b) I (c) you (d) residents (e) mother

G3 THE PRESENT PERFECT TENSE

1. A. (a) have cleaned (b) changed (c) has appointed (d) have been (e) wrote
   B. (a) have been found (b) has been collected (c) were repaired (d) have been introduced (e) was seen.

2. A. (a) has lost (b) have been involved (c) has fallen off (d) have been demolished (e) has rained.
   B. (a) has improved (b) has been destroyed (c) have sprung up (d) have risen (e) have been brought

Answers

3. (a) have been standing
   (b) has been trying
   (c) has been working
   (d) have been watching
   (e) has been feeding

G4 THE PAST PERFECT TENSE

2. (a) The government had been overthrown by rebel forces.
   (b) A young man had been seen prowling around the house two days before the fire.
   (c) Her money had been stolen by the electrician.
   (d) Livestock had also been destroyed by the water.
   (e) We had been advised by the foreman to report for work on that day.

3. (a) had been (b) reappeared (c) joined (d) had won (e) had seen

4. (a) Mr Singh replied that the Ministry of Works had spent thousands of dollars on widening the Cumana Road.
   (b) Brian complained that those children wasted too much water.
   (c) The bulletin states that only one of the Siamese twins has survived the operation.
   (d) Her brother explained that she had done it just to tease her boyfriend.
   (e) The counter clerk announced that Flight 327 was already boarding.

G5 THE PASSIVE VOICE

1. A. (a) His work is admired by people all over the world.
   (b) Meals are provided by the school for underprivileged children.
   (c) She is expected to arrive tomorrow.
   (d) Their judgement in these matters is always influenced by their political allegiance.
   (e) Bags of garbage are left everywhere

   B. (a) A limited area of the country was put under curfew.
   (b) Their houses were built entirely out of indigenous materials.
   (c) This year the crown was taken by a new and little-known calypsonian.
   (d) Two of the accident victims were pronounced dead on arrival.
   (e) The hostages were released one by one to a waiting crowd.

C. (a) The price of beer has been lowered by competition between the two breweries.
   (b) By then the results of the Common Entrance Examination had already been published.
   (c) These events will be remembered by our people for a long time to come.
   (d) This expense cannot be justified.
   (e) An emergency plan must be presented by the sub-committee within twenty-four hours.

2. A. (a) need to be inspected
      (b) need to be repaired
      (c) need to be painted
      (d) need to be renovated
      (e) need to be sprayed

   B. (a) continue to be fired
      (b) continue to be hired
      (c) continue to be redeployed
      (d) continue to be victimized
      (e) continue to be recruited

   C. (a) seems to have been done
      (b) seems to have been decided
      (c) seems to have been moved
      (d) seems to have been disturbed
      (e) seems to have been changed

   D. (a) are known to be stolen
      (b) are known to be imported
      (c) are known to be destroyed
      (d) are known to be distributed
      (e) are known to be produced

   E. (a) were thought to have harboured
      (b) were said to have harboured
      (c) were known to have harboured
      (d) were alleged to have harboured
      (e) were reported to have harboured

3. A. (a) cannot be condoned
      (b) which are at present being experienced
      (c) children need to be corrected
      (d) have been changed
      (e) will only be reduced

   B. (a) should be rectified
      (b) has been gained
      (c) you are asked to demonstrate hand signals and do a hill test
      (d) it is hoped; is being experienced
      (e) that could be recycled

   C. (a) should be abandoned
      (b) students are not supposed
      (c) will not be satisfied
      (d) maintained
      (e) depressed

Answers

G6 NOTABLE PAST PARTICIPLES

1. (a) All kinds of goods are laid out on the pavement.
    (b) The school is run like a military operation.
    (c) The National Anthem is sung at all public functions.
    (d) In this game five points are lost for each incorrect response.
    (e) Between 3.00 and 3.15 p.m. government notices are broadcast by the radio station.

2. (a) Structural Adjustment policies have led
    (b) This mirror has never lied.
    (c) Patients have lain here
    (d) New musical forms have begun
    (e) The bell has rung

G7 VERBS ENDING WITH D, T OR N

1. (a) Their machinery is treated with great care.
    (b) Little children are frightened by some masqueraders.
    (c) Your statement is regarded as an ultimatum.
    (d) Our hearts are saddened by such events.
    (e) These sudden changes are rejected by the older people.

2. (a) Participants have adopted
    (b) The landlord has often threatened
    (c) Mildew has blackened
    (d) The new development has actually strengthened
    (e) Talks between the two parties have inevitably ended

3. (a) affected (b) worsened (c) broadened (d) built (e) disconnected.

H1 THE PRESENT PARTICIPLE AS NOUN AND ADJECTIVE

3. A. (a) widening - noun   (b) antagonizing - noun
   (c) waving - adjective   (d) cleaning - noun
   (e) following - adjective

B. (a) pretending - adjective
(b) climbing - noun
(c) mounting - adjective
(d) surrounding - adjective
(e) ironing - noun

C. (a) graduating - adjective
(b) using - noun
(c) setting - noun
(d) representing - adjective
(e) meddling - noun

H2 THE CONTINUOUS TENSES

2. A. (a) is being investigated
(b) is being taken up
(c) is being reopened
(d) is being documented
(e) is being monitored

B. (a) are being sponsored
(b) are being chosen
(c) are being screened
(d) are being outfitted
(e) are being prepared

C. (a) am being promoted
(b) am being redeployed
(c) am being moved
(d) am being appointed
(e) am being demoted

D. (a) was being demolished
(b) was being renovated
(c) was being refurbished
(d) was being rewired
(e) was being fumigated

E. (a) were being examined
(b) were being studied
(c) were being discussed
(d) were being weighed
(e) were being entertained

3. (a) All the old, historic buildings were being torn down.

(b) You are being manipulated by your child.

(c) I am not being paid overtime.

(d) Taxpayers' money is being wasted on this project.

(e) Children under 12 were not being admitted.

4. (a) were not having/weren't having

(b) was not walking/wasn't walking

(c) are not being renewed/aren't being renewed

(d) has not been feeding/hasn't been feeding

(e) is not being raised/isn't being raised

Answers

5. (a) Were they having a good time?
    (b) Was she walking along Davies Street?
    (c) Are their contracts being renewed?
    (d) Has Nnamdi been feeding the animals?
    (e) Is the price of flour being raised?

6. (a) Weren't they having a good time?
    (b) Wasn't she walking along Davies Street?
    (c) Aren't their contracts being renewed?
    (d) Hasn't Nnamdi been feeding the animals?
    (e) Isn't the price of flour being raised?

H3 CONFUSING THE PARTICIPLES

1. (a) interested (b) depressing (c) bored (d) confused (e) exciting

3. A. (a) being attacked (b) being ridiculed (c) being chased
       (d) being victimized (e) being fleeced
   B. (a) having been interrogated (b) having been detained
      (c) having been welcomed (d) having been intimidated
      (e) having been cautioned
   C. (a) were being paid (b) were being briefed
      (c) were being warned (d) were being recruited
      (e) were being photographed
   D. (a) having been influenced (b) having been subverted
      (c) having been discouraged (d) having been dissuaded
      (e) having been distracted
   E. (a) being released (b) being convicted (c) being hired
      (d) being appointed (e) being indicted

4. (a) being (b) been (c) been (d) being (e) being

5. (a) frustrated (b) overflowing (c) being (d) resulting (e) lighted

273

Index

adjectival nouns, 86-8
adjectives, 8-10, 27, 86-8, 192-6, 224-7
adverbs, 16-18, 20, 28, 202
apostrophe, 77-85, 133, 151-2, 167
are, See is and are
articles, definite and indefinite, 61-7
auxiliaries, 13, 129-36, 197, 202; modal, 142-3, 179-89, 209, 227-9

be, to be, 101-5, 173-9, 227-38
been and being, 229-38
being, See been and being

clauses, 33, 116-9. See also if-clauses; main; subordinate

complements, 39-42.
conditional sentences, 178-9, 182-5, 187-8
conjunctions, 22-3, 28-9
continuous (or progressive) tenses, 227-32
contractions, 133-6, 151-3, 166-8, 174, 181, 185, 197
could and would, 179-89
could have and would have, 182-5, 188
countable and uncountable nouns, 58-65, 74-6, 68
creole grammar, 56, 61-2, 76, 83, 87, 99, 102-3, 112, 113-14, 128,133-4, 136-7, 140, 148, 151, 154, 158, 164, 166, 175, 180, 183, 192, 198-9, 210, 218, 228

determiners, 25, 60-5
did and didn't, 164-8
direct and indirect speech. See reported speech

direct object, 34-7
do, does, don't, doesn't, 128-42
double negatives, 136-9, 152, 153, 166-7

either and neither, 121-2
en ending, 190, 220-2

finite and non-finite verbs, 12-13, 31

had, 202-8
have and has, 91, 113-14, 197-201
head word/head noun, 105-9

I, 174-5
if-clauses, 178-9
imperative mood, 14
indicative mood, 14
indirect object, 37-8
indirect speech. See reported speech.
infinitive, 12, 129, 142-7, 168-72
interjections, 23-4, 29
interrogative (or question) forms, 14, 128-31, 164-5, 173-4, 181, 185, 197, 210, 228
intransitive verbs. See transitive and intransitive verbs,
inversion, 112-15
irregular verbs, 156-61, 215-20
is and are, 101-5

lay and lie, 217-18
linking verbs, 39-40
loose, lose, loss, lost, 219-20

main clause, 43-7
mass nouns, 58-60
modal auxiliaries. See auxiliaries

Index

modifiers, modify, 8-10, 17-19, 27, 28, 45, 86-8, 191-6, 224-7, 232-3, 234-5
mood, 14. See also subjunctive mood

negative, 132-42, 151-5, 166-8, 174, 181, 185, 197, 210, 213, 228
neither. See either and neither
nouns, 3-5, 25-6, 51-88.
number, 51-76

object, 19, 34-8, 208-19.
object complement, 40-1

participles, 12, 190-238

parts of speech, 3-29
passive voice, 200, 208-15, 227, 229
past participle, 190-222, 232-8
past perfect (or pluperfect) tense, 182-3, 202-8
past simple tense, 156-79
person, first, second and third person, 96
phrases, 42-8, 105-10. See also prepositional phrases
pluperfect tense. See past perfect tense
plural. See singular and plural
possessive nouns, 77-88
prepositional phrases, 19-22, 33
prepositions, 19-22, 28
present participle, 223-38
present perfect tense, 197-201
present simple tense, 91-155
progressive tenses. See continuous tenses
pronouns, 5-8, 26, 173, 174-5. See also relative pronouns
punctuation, 46, 47-8. See also apostrophe

quantity expressions, 67-72, 119-25
question forms. See interrogative forms

relative pronouns, 116-19
reported speech, 203-5
sentences, 30-48
sequence of tenses, 204-8
singular and plural, 51-76
subject, 30-34
subject complement, 39-40
subject-verb agreement, 95-127, 129-36, 140-55, 173-8, 197, 209, 229
subjunctive mood, 14, 144, 170-1, 178-9
subordinate clauses, 44-8, 107, 116-19
subordinators, 44
substitution table (how to use), 97

tense, 13-4. See also individual tenses in sections E-H.
there is, there are, 113-15
transitive and intransitive verbs, 36, 40, 208-9
uncountable nouns. See countable and uncountable nouns

verbs, 11-16, 27, 30-1, 35, 91-238
voice, 14. See also passive voice

was and were, 173-9
will, 179-81, 185
word classes, See parts of speech
word slots, 24-9
would. See could and would.
would have. See could have and would have.
you, 173

www.ingramcontent.com/pod-product-compliance
Ingram Content Group UK Ltd.
Pitfield, Milton Keynes, MK11 3LW, UK
UKHW041952230426
12048UKWH00008B/293